*The Intelligible
Constitution*

The Intelligible Constitution

The Supreme Court's Obligation
to Maintain the Constitution
as Something We the People
Can Understand

JOSEPH GOLDSTEIN

OXFORD UNIVERSITY PRESS
New York   Oxford

Oxford University Press

Oxford   New York
Athens   Auckland   Bangkok   Bombay
Calcutta   Cape Town   Dar es Salaam   Delhi
Florence   Hong Kong   Istanbul   Karachi
Kuala Lumpur   Madras   Madrid   Melbourne
Mexico City   Nairobi   Paris   Singapore
Taipei   Tokyo   Toronto

and associated companies in
Berlin   Ibadan

Copyright © 1992 by Oxford University Press, Inc.

First published in 1992 by Oxford University Press, Inc.,
198 Madison Avenue, New York, New York 10016

First issued as an Oxford University Press paperback, 1995

Oxford is a registered trademark of Oxford University Press

All rights reserved. No part of this publication may be reproduced,
stored in a retrieval system, or transmitted, in any form or by any means,
electronic, mechanical, photocopying, recording, or otherwise,
without the prior permission of Oxford University Press.

Library of Congress Cataloging-in-Publication Data
Goldstein, Joseph.
The intelligible Constitution :
the Supreme Court's obligation
to maintain the constitution
as something we the people can understand
/ Joseph Goldstein.   p.   cm.
Includes bibliographical references and index.
ISBN 0-19-507328-2
ISBN 0-19-509375-5 (Pbk.)
1. United States. Supreme Court.
2. United States—Constitutional law—Interpretation and construction.
3. Judicial opinions—United States.
I. Title.
KF8742G65   1992   347.73'26—dc20   [347.30735]   91-26709

2 4 6 8 10 9 7 5 3 1

Printed in the United States of America

For Sonja

ACKNOWLEDGMENTS

With thanks and appreciation I acknowledge the following persons for the many ways—more than they may realize—in which they contributed to the development of this book: Bruce A. Ackerman, Akhil R. Amar, Valerie Aubry, Aharon Barak, Guido Calabresi, Anupam Chander, Stephen C. Chin, Gene P. Coakley, Morris L. Cohen, Stephen A. Conrad, Walter E. Dellinger III, Jean Doherty, Paul S. Feira, Daniel J. Freed, Sonja Goldstein, Stephen Goldstein, Alan L. Hirsch, Riyaz A. Kanji, Alexander Kogan, Andrew Marovitz, Burke Marshall, Helen McInnis, Norman C. Oder, Paul Oetken, Irene Pavitt, Robert S. Peck, H. Jefferson Powell, Henry Putzel, Jr., Heather Quay, Charles A. Reich, Bernard Schwartz, Fred Shapiro, Michael Solender, Carole Solis-Cohen, Philip Tegeler, Gayle Van Dole, Ruth G. Wedgwood, and Joshua Weisman.

I promised myself when I began studying Constitutional Law in 1976, with Small Groups of first-term students in seminar, that I would not write on the subject for at least a decade. I also decided to use as teaching materials the complete opinions in Supreme Court cases concerned with the meaning of the Constitution rather than the edited fare of traditional casebooks. Together with my students, I have sought to learn to read, to understand, and to assess these unpruned opinions as communications about the Constitution.

What happened in the Small Groups determined the nature of this book, which first began to take visible shape during the spring of 1987. At that time four students from my 1986 Group (who came to call themselves "The Marshall Clan" and whose names are listed above)—joined me on a regular basis over sandwiches in my office to fashion questions and to think about Chief Justice Marshall's admonition in *McCulloch v. Maryland* that "we must never forget, that it is *a constitution* we are expounding."

My students have always been my teachers. I am indebted to them for their critical, constructive, and unrelenting challenges. I acknowledge particularly the contribution of the members of the 1988 and 1989 Groups who read near-final drafts of the manuscript and who let me know their thoughts.

Finally, I thank specifically five students, all included in the list above, for the special part each played in our intense elbow-to-elbow relationship while preparing the manuscript for publication. They are Anupam Chander, Paul S. Feira, Riyaz A. Kanji, Norman C. Oder, and Paul Oetken.

New Haven, Conn.   J.G.
June 1991

CONTENTS

Part III   CANONS OF
                 COMPREHENSIBILITY

A FOREWORD

In the usual note that appears before the opinions of members of the Supreme Court in *Arizona v. Fulminante*, 111 S.Ct. 1246 (1991), delivered on March 26, 1991, it is stated:

> WHITE, J., delivered an opinion, Parts I, II, and IV of which are for the Court, and filed a dissenting opinion in Part III. MARSHALL, BLACKMUN, and STEVENS, JJ., joined Parts I, II, III, and IV of that opinion; SCALIA, J., joined Parts I and II; and KENNEDY, J., joined Parts I and IV. REHNQUIST, C.J., delivered an opinion, Part II of which is for the Court, and filed a dissenting opinion in Parts I and III. O'CONNOR, J., joined Parts I, II, and III of that opinion; KENNEDY and SOUTER, JJ., joined Parts I and II; and SCALIA, J., joined Parts II and III. KENNEDY, J., filed an opinion concurring in the judgment.

The Court decided, contrary to precedent, that admission of a coerced confession in a criminal trial could, in appropriate cases, be treated as "harmless error," not requiring reversal of a conviction. Five members of the Court thought so. Another five thought that even if this were the appropriate rule, it did not apply to Fulminante's conviction. Four members, however, thought that the confession was not coerced anyway, making it unnecessary for them to reach the "harmless error" question, even though they did so. One of these thought that since five members apparently (as to one of them the matter is somewhat murky, to say the least) believed the confession to have been coerced, even though he himself did not, he should go ahead and decide whether its admission was "harmless error." He concluded that it was not, formulating in the process a unique standard of "harmless error" for such occasions with which no one else expressed agreement.

If this is confusing, remember that the work of the Court in the *Fulminante* case, as is true of many cases, was of direct operative interest not only to the lower federal and state courts throughout the land, but also to all the principal actors in the criminal justice system, especially prosecutors, defense counsel, and police officials, everywhere. It is to this problem of the Court as communicator, of its educational function so to speak, that Professor Joseph Goldstein of the Yale Law School has addressed himself in this provocative and often deliberately disturbing book.

In doing so, Goldstein departs dramatically from the norm of literature on constitutional law and history, and thus makes a unique and important contribution to it.

Unlike the work of teachers like Alexander Bickel, Charles Black, John Ely, Cass Sunstein, and Harry Wellington, for example, Goldstein's book is not about theories of interpreting the Constitution—that is to say, he does not purport to instruct the Court how to go about its substantive constitutional work. Further, unlike other works dealing with specific constitutional problems such as those associated with race (of which there are almost innumerable examples), or arising under the Speech Clause (books by Lee Bollinger, Zechariah Chafee, Kent Greenawalt, or Frederick Schauer, for instance) or the Religion Clauses (as in the writings of Mark De Wolfe Howe, Philip Kurland, or Leo Pfeffer), this book does not analyze, from either a doctrinal or historical point of view, a particular body of the Court's work. It is instead about "expounding" the Constitution (to use Goldstein's favorite verb from his favorite opinion, that of John Marshall in *McCulloch v. Maryland*)—that is, explaining it to the people—in any of a variety of contexts.

The cases that form the instrument of Goldstein's thesis are familiar, at least for the most part, not only to constitutional lawyers, but to the reading public at large. Three of them—the *Brown* cases, *Cooper v. Aaron*, and *Bakke*—are pivotal markers in the progression of American law and society from one of institutionalized racism toward the ideal, if not always the fact, of equality under law. Another—the *Webster* case, which is discussed peripherally in the opening chapter as a stark contrast to Marshall's *McCulloch* opinion—is illustrative of the deep division in the Court about the constitutional scope, indeed the constitutional existence, of a woman's right to reproductive choice, in the context of abortion technology. In his discussion of this case, Goldstein uses the headnote from the Court's decision to illustrate a judicial doctrinal chaos similar to that of the *Fulminante* case noted at the start of this Foreword. Finally, and somewhat more arcane, there is a full treatment of the jagged path of the so far short-lived judicially created constitutional constraint on congressional power under the Commerce Clause to control the decisions of state and local governments with respect to labor standards, such as those concerned with wages and hours.

All these cases have been the subject of intensive academic and judicial scrutiny elsewhere, but not of the kind or order that they are given in the book. What Goldstein is concerned with is unexplained ambiguity, not the merits of the Court's, or the individual justices', substantive views on the constitutional issues raised by the cases. Each of the case studies was chosen for a different kind of ambiguity; that in the *Brown* set and in *Cooper v. Aaron*, for example, is concealed in unanimous opinions, whereas those in the other examples are a consequence (not the only consequence) of fundamental differences among the justices in approach and as to outcome.

There are, of course, explanations for the ambiguities. The disjunction between the identification of the right of the plaintiffs in *Brown I* and the delayed remedy in *Brown II*, which apparently denied to individual plaintiffs any actual achievement of the rights previously proclaimed, can be said to be a direct result of the persistent confusion in equal protection jurisprudence as to whether the Court's concern was essentially with the structure of school districts, and group rights, or with judicial enforcement of personal rights that could be realized individual by individual. The same is true of the unexplained switch from the use of the word "integration" by the lower courts in *Cooper v. Aaron* to the word "desegregation" in the opinion of the Supreme Court, signed by all nine justices, but drafted by Justice Brennan, and described here in Chapter 3. It was not until years later that the Court clearly identified the school boards' constitutional obligation as one to eliminate all vestiges of prior dual system's "root and branch," and the corresponding constitutional right as one to attend a school district in which that had been accomplished, rather than merely a right not to be denied access to a particular school of one's choice because of one's race.

Since to do so is part of my profession, I can deliver explanations for the ambiguities in the book's other opinion studies as well. But that is just the problem for Professor Goldstein. The Court has either deliberately or inadvertently left it to me and to the authors referred to earlier and to Goldstein himself, if he chose to do so, to fill in the blanks, to explain the obscure, to construct for our students and for the people generally what it is that the Court surely meant,

when the Court itself does not say what it meant. Goldstein knows as well as I that what I have said in the
previous paragraph is a possible, or possibly even a
probable, explanation of the Court's ambivalence in the
early race cases as to exactly what it was deciding. His
conviction, however, is that the Court itself has an obligation to strive to discern and articulate the reasons
for its ambivalence, even if it is unable to resolve it at
a particular time, in a particular decision. This conviction is the basis, the rationale, for the five "canons of
comprehensibility" set forth in the concluding chapter.
That chapter, and the book, are a plea for a deliberate,
institutional commitment by the Court, by all its members as a body, to bring simplicity, candor, clarity, mu-
tual fairness, and textual integrity to the opinions both
of the Court and of the individual justices concurring
and dissenting, such that failures to decide, inability to
agree, and the essential elements of disagreement are
brought to the surface and exposed not by the innumerable commentators on the Court's work, but by the
Court itself.

   If this sounds simple, let me assure you that it is
not. On the contrary, it bristles with premises—articles
of faith, really, for they are not based on experience
with the Court's work, at least in this century—about
the nature and function of the judicial branch, and of
the justices' individual and joint jobs.

   One such premise, it seems to me, is that the opinions of the Supreme Court, and of all its members, can
be and therefore should be comprehensible to every-

one. It is to say the least doubtful that this is a premise shared by the justices. They may profess the belief, if asked, that their work should be accessible to the lower courts, to the other parts of the national government, to the instrumentalities of the states, to the legal academy, and to the bar. Yet the evidence of experience suggests that even this may not be so; often the justices appear to be talking mainly to one another, as in the *Webster* case and the *National League–Garcia* line, discussed in the book. Familiarity with the Court's work overwhelmingly demonstrates at a minimum that the members of the Court view their work as directed at the elite, and not to the people.

This fact, which I believe to be accepted without cavil by Court experts, conflicts directly with another underlying premise of the book. That premise is that a necessary justification for judicial review—for the Court's power to say that government cannot do what the people acting through their elected representatives want it to do—is the Court's ability to explain in each case in a way that the people as the sovereign can understand what it is in the Constitution that forbids (or, in the opposite case, permits) government to take the contested action. This simple notion of the relationship between the Court as interpreter of the Constitution and the people as the source of consent, of the grant of the power of final interpretation to the Court, is as basic a notion of the limits of justified judicial review as is, say, the doctrine of original intent as a constraint, recently embraced by some, or as the notion of the Constitution as the embodiment of fundamental values and rights as a rule of law.

Another premise, or so it also seems to me, is that ambivalences and ambiguities of the sort described in the book can be exposed, explained, and made clear without a consensus among the justices, or at least a majority of them, with respect to the constitutional doctrine or principles at stake. A basis for this premise must be that the justices' job is to act as a cohort of teachers, of rational decision-makers, who can agree on a coherent statement of the source and dimensions of whatever disagreements they have. The justices should not, in other words, attempt to persuade others, outside the Court, as to what the Court believes the path of the law should be, or what the decision in the case at hand suggests it will be, unless at least a majority of the justices agree on those points. This vision of how the justices should act is the source of Professor Goldstein's principled criticism of Justice Brennan's statement in the *Bakke* case, for four members of the Court only, of what they thought was "the central meaning" of the opinions filed in that case. Goldstein does not suggest that the Justice, or any of the three who joined his opinion, did not truly believe that they were correctly interpreting the other opinions, especially that of Justice Powell, but only that a statement with such important implications should not have been made without qualification. Obviously this raises the question what the four signing the Brennan concurrence thought their job was. I believe that they thought it was to persuade the Court in future cases, and lower courts, as to what the proper contitutional rule was as a consequence of the *Bakke* decision itself, not only what it should be. As the book shows, that result in fact occurred in some lower courts, and I think it a fair statement that the "central meaning" characterization, not just of the *Bakke* case itself, but of the affirmative action issue, has stood the test of time. The question, however, is the propriety of the unarguably common practice of the justices in their opinions of arguing a point of view, rather than dispassionately, rationally, analyzing the perhaps temporary inability of the Court to reach one.

It is possible that Professor Goldstein's thesis can be viewed as instrumental in nature—that is to say, that clarity and candor in the Supreme Court's work will in turn cause the constitutional system to function better, to help make, as the justices said at the end of their opinion in *Cooper v. Aaron,* the rule of law "a living truth." Certainly much of the analysis of the judicial function by other authors is in that vein. The question about *Brown* and *Cooper v. Aaron,* for example, would be whether events in later years, and the prospects of implementing the great principles of *Brown,* would have been eased by bringing to light rather than submerging the enormously difficult undecided issues in those cases. But I do not believe that is what Professor Goldstein is about. I believe he is about provoking debate and discussion regarding the Supreme Court's deepest functions in expounding the Constitution in a democratic society. I believe that his underlying premise is that the Court as an institution, and the members of the Court individually, have a preeminent duty of principled explanation of what is actually going on in constitutional decision-making, and that it and they have lost sight of that duty. This is a book that takes the sovereignty of the people literally and seriously, and derives from that their right to be told what is going on, and why, in the judicial branch.

Burke Marshall
Nicholas deB. Katzenbach
Professor of Law
Yale Law School
New Haven, Conn.

PART I

WHY AN INTELLIGIBLE CONSTITUTION

CHAPTER 1

MADE FOR AN UNDEFINED FUTURE*

"[W]e must never forget, that it is *a constitution* we are expounding." So wrote Chief Justice John Marshall in 1819 for a unanimous Supreme Court in *McCulloch v. Maryland*.[1] What should be the impact of *McCulloch's* "never forget" admonition on the opinion-writing task of the justices engaged in expounding the Constitution? What is it about that instrument that they should never forget, and why? What demands do the answers to this intertwined what-and-why question make on them? By what criteria, by what canons of style, should their

---

*"The Constitution of the United States ... was made for an undefined and expanding future, and for a people gathered and to be gathered from many nations and of many tongues." *Hurtado v. California*, 110 U.S. 516, 530–531 (1884) (Matthews, J., Opinion of the Court).

opinions be assessed as communications about the Constitution, whether they be majority, concurring, or dissenting? These are the questions that this book addresses.

I

Answers to these questions rest on some understanding of what a constitution is. The *McCulloch* Court tied its "never forget" admonition to the importance of remembering that the Constitution "derives its whole authority" from the people; that it is meant to govern "their posterity"; that it is intended "to be adapted to various *crises* of human affairs" as they occur; and that, in form and language, it is an instrument designed to be accessible and comprehensible to the "public," We the People of every generation.[2]

Concerned with *what* the justices as the expositors of the Constitution must keep in mind about it, the Court said:

> A constitution, to contain an accurate detail of all the subdivisions of which its great powers will admit, and of all the means by which they may be carried into execution, would partake of the prolixity of a legal code, and could scarcely be embraced by the human mind. It probably would never be understood by the public. Its nature, therefore, requires, that only its great outlines should be marked, its important objects designated,* and the minor

---

*Justice Marshall's characterization of the Constitution does not apply

ingredients which compose those objects be deduced from the nature of the objects themselves.[3]

Stressing the simple-understandable-language and the great-outline characteristics of the Constitution, the *McCulloch* Court emphasized that "the people were at perfect liberty to accept or reject it"; that "the necessity of referring it to the people, and of deriving its powers directly from them, was felt and acknowledged by all"; and that "the people have, in express terms, [said] 'this constitution, and the laws of the United States, which shall be made in pursuance thereof,' 'shall be the supreme law of the land.' "[4]

By connecting its "never forget" words to its expounding function, the *McCulloch* Court could have been telling itself and future Courts that its communications *on behalf of* and *to* We the People who "decided" to establish the Constitution must be something that We can understand if We are to remain sovereign, if Our consent to the government is to be sustained.[5] As Thomas Jefferson observed, there is "no safe depository of the ultimate powers of the society but the people themselves: and if we think them not enlightened enough to exercise their control with a wholesome discretion, the remedy is not to take it from them, but to inform their discretion."[6] Accepting that We the

---

to all its parts. For example, requirements that senators "have attained to the Age of thirty Years" (art. I, § 3) or that the president be "a natural born Citizen" (art. II, § 1) are code-like in their specificity. Contrariwise, legislation may contain constitution-like general provisions to guide the promulgation and enforcement of specific rules and regulations.

People of every generation are responsible for maintaining and, if necessary, amending Our Constitution, which "is intended to endure for ages," the Court must inform Our discretion when it decides cases in which there is a controversy about the Constitution's meaning.[7]

If Ours is to be an "intelligent democracy," if Our revolutions are to be peaceful, We the People, the *McCulloch* Court implicitly recognized, must be able to learn, from Our own reading of the Constitution and the Supreme Court's constructions of it, what rights We have and do not have, what values are and are not protected, and what limits are and are not imposed on those who govern on Our behalf.[8] For then We can meet Our responsibility as informed citizens to respond to what the Court did and why it did it.*

The Court's constitutional law is, as binding precedent, effectively the supreme law of the land until the Court overrules itself or is overruled by amendment.[9] Whether We the People retain "an unenumerated right to amend our Constitution in ways not explicitly set out in Article V"[10] or are restricted by that Article to

---

*"[The] Court was faithful to the democratic tradition [when it] wrote in words that all could understand why it did what it did. That is vital to the integrity of the judicial process." W. Douglas, Stare Decisis: *Eighth Annual Benjamin N. Cardozo Lecture to the Association of the Bar of the City of New York* (1949), 12.

"[W]e must do our utmost to make clear and easily understandable the reasons for deciding these cases as we do. Forthright observance of rights presupposes their forthright definition." *Douglas v. Jeannette*, 319 U.S. 157, 182 (1943) (Jackson, J., concurring).

accepting or rejecting amendments through our representatives in Congress and our state legislature or through delegates We send to a "Convention for proposing Amendments,"[11] the Court is obligated to provide in its communications to Us, the governed and the governors, a basis for discovering "faults" in the Constitution and for deliberating and deciding whether to speak out and to seek the correction of its "errors" in controversy before the Court or by amendment.[12] That is *why* Our justices on the Court must never forget that the Constitution, which they expound, emanated from Us, was meant to remain comprehensible to Us, and was established for Our posterity to endure and to be modified with Our informed consent.

II

How should judicial opinions interpreting the Constitution be fashioned to meet the "never forget" admonition? How should they be read? In *McCulloch*, Chief Justice Marshall stressed that to be "understood by the public," a constitution must, for the most part, in form and in language, provide only the "great outlines of government" and "its important objects."[13] At the same time, he recognized that "[s]uch is the character of human language, that no word conveys to the mind, in all situations, one single definite idea."[14] The burden of an opinion is to remove obstacles to understanding when a controversy arises between or among the governors and the governed about the meaning of the Constitution. The Court's task must be to make comprehensible provisions of the Constitution whose language has conveyed different meanings to different minds. This should not obscure the fact that the language of opinions may be no more free of ambiguity than the language of constitutional provisions. Nevertheless, the Court's task of explaining, of giving reasons for its judgment in a concrete case, is to clarify—to make something about the Constitution more fully understood than it was before the opinion was rendered.[15]

Further, in formulating constitutional principles on which to rest its decisions, the Court should strive to maintain the character of the instrument. It must avoid changing the nature of the Constitution. It must not convert it into a detailed body of rules and regulations. It must not forget that in expounding the Constitution, the constitutional principles it constructs are "intended to endure for ages to come, and, consequently, to be adapted to the various *crises* of human affairs."[16]

Implicit in the "never forget" admonition is that the Court in fashioning constitutional principles has a task not unlike the drafting task given to the Committees of Detail and Style of the Constitutional Convention of 1787. A working document written by Edmund Randolph and used by the Committee of Detail entitled "Draft Sketch of Constitution" provided the following guidelines:

In the draught of a fundamental constitution, two things deserve attention:

1. To insert essential principles only; lest the operations of government should be clogged by rendering those provisions permanent and unalterable, which ought to be accommodated to times and events: and

2. To use simple and precise language, and general propositions, according to the example of the (several) constitutions of the several states. (For the construction of a constitution necessarily differs from that of law).[17]

The *McCulloch* Court, sensitive to these notions, observed:

To have prescribed the means by which government should, in all future time, execute its powers, would have been to change, entirely, the character of the instrument, and give it the properties of a legal code. It would have been an unwise attempt to provide, by immutable rules, for exigencies which, if foreseen at all, must have been seen dimly, and which can be best provided for as they occur.[18]

Maintaining the distinction between means and objects, between rules and principles, is essential to maintaining the character of the Constitution. For the Court to approve, much less prescribe, means without identifying the constitutional provisions or principles on which its decisions rest or for the Court to be principleless in its expounding of the Constitution would be to risk gradually depriving it of its accessibility and timelessness.

III

The magnificently crafted opinion in *McCulloch v. Maryland* is remembered not because the Court upheld Congress's power to incorporate a bank of the United States and denied Maryland the power to tax a branch of that bank. The opinion is remembered for what it contributes to our understanding of the Constitution, particularly the texts of Article I, Section 8, authorizing Congress "[t]o make all Laws which shall be necessary and proper for carrying into Execution the ... Powers vested by this Constitution in the Government of the United States";[19] of Article VI, establishing the authority of the national government as a sovereign body in relation to the authority of a state as a sovereign body by making the "Constitution, and Laws of the United States ... the Supreme Law of the Land [notwithstanding] any Thing in the Constitution or Laws of any State to the Contrary"; and of the Tenth Amendment, which provides that "[t]he powers not delegated to the United States by the Constitution, nor prohibited by it to the States, are reserved to the States respectively."[20]

The Court determined first that Congress had the power to establish a national bank. The opinion explained, as Professor Gunther has summarized it,

that the Bank was constitutional because the Constitution should be broadly and flexibly interpreted, because one could not expect such a document to specify every power that the national government might properly exert, because one should not be miserly in finding implied national powers, because Congress legitimately had broad discretion in selecting means to achieve the ends listed in the recital of delegated national powers in the Constitution.[21]

With these propositions established about the nature of the Constitution and how it should be read, the Court formulated a constitutional principle, designed to enhance public understanding and to "endure for the ages to come": "Let the end [of the national legislature's action] be legitimate, let it be within the scope of the constitution, and all means which are appropriate, which are plainly adapted to that end, which are not prohibited, but consistent with the letter and spirit of the constitution, are constitutional."[22]

Likewise, in deciding that Maryland, as a sovereign body, could not tax the nation's bank, the Court kept in mind that it was expounding a constitution "in its most interesting and vital parts."[23] The "conflicting powers of the government of the Union and of its members, as marked [only in great outline] in that constitution" had to be addressed.[24] After acknowledging "[t]hat the power of taxation is one of vital importance; that it is retained by the States; [and] that it is not abridged by the grant of a similar power to the government of the Union," the Court focused on what was in dispute about the meaning of the Constitution.[25] It said, asked, and replied:

The sovereignty of a State extends to everything which
exists by its own authority, or is introduced by its permission; but does it extend to those *means* which are
employed by Congress to carry into execution powers
conferred on that body by the people of the United States?
We think it demonstrable that it does not. Those powers
are not given by the people of a single State. They are
given by the people of the United States. . . . Consequently,
the people of a single State cannot confer a sovereignty
which will extend over them.[26]

. . .

The legislature of the Union alone, therefore, can be
trusted by the people with the power of controlling measures which concern all, in the confidence that it will not
be abused.[27]

Thus the *McCulloch* Court provided a model for
expounding the Constitution. It gave meaning to the
task that justices of the Supreme Court confront when
addressing cases and controversies about what the
Constitution permits, requires, or prohibits. It rested
its decisions about the constitutionality of specific
claims on constitutional principles of general application. Recognizing that no provisions of the Constitution
expressly answer these claims, the Court fashioned "intelligible" principles that maintain its great outlines.
Each of the principles enhances our understanding of
the Constitution. Each, it would seem, "so entirely per-
vades the constitution, is so intermixed with the materials which compose it, so interwoven with its web,

so blended with its texture, as to be incapable of being separated from it, without rendering it into shreds."[28]

IV

The justices, seeking to find "fair and just interpretation[s]," do not always keep firmly in mind—indeed, may not always be able to keep in mind—the distinction between means and objects, between minor ingredients and constitutional principles.[29] This seems to be especially true with regard to the *means*—rules and remedies—established not by legislative or administrative bodies, but by the Court itself. The *McCulloch* Court in 1819 distinguished with clarity constitutional *principles* from legislatively fashioned *means*. In contrast, the 1989 Court, with its six opinions in *Webster v. Reproductive Health Services*, left its readers confused about whether the "trimester framework" that it had fashioned in *Roe v. Wade* for determining the constitutionality of abortion laws was to be perceived and assessed as a constitutional *principle* or merely a *means* for preserving the constitutional right to privacy.[30]

The *Roe* framework provides, it would seem in code-like fashion, that "to approximately the end of the first trimester, the abortion decision and its effectuation must be left to the medical judgment of the pregnant woman's attending physician," that following "the end of the first trimester, the State, in promoting its interest in the health of the mother, may . . . regulate the abortion procedure in ways that are reasonably related to maternal health," and "subsequent to viability, the State in promoting its interest in the potentiality of human life may . . . proscribe . . . abortion except where it is necessary . . . for the preservation of the life or health of the mother."[31] Chief Justice Rehnquist, writing for a plurality in *Webster*—there was no majority—declared:

> [T]he rigid *Roe* framework is hardly consistent with the notion of a Constitution cast in general terms, as ours is, and usually speaking in general principles, as ours does. The key elements of the *Roe* framework—trimesters and viability—are not found in the text of the Constitution or in any place else one would expect to find a constitutional principle. . . . [T]he result has been a web of legal rules that have become increasingly intricate, resembling a code of regulations rather than a body of constitutional doctrine.[32]

Chief Justice Rehnquist failed to acknowledge that the *Roe* framework is not necessarily incompatible with the notion of a constitution cast in general terms, so long as it is perceived as a means and not an end. Thus the question is not whether the framework constitutes "a code of regulations rather than a body of constitutional doctrine," but whether as a code of regulations it is "consistent with the letter and spirit of the Constitution."[33] More specifically, the question is whether the framework is unsound in principle or too complex to be understandable and workable in practice when states and courts use it as a guide in balancing the privacy rights of individuals in obtaining abortions against other competing constitutional interests. It is a rule, not a general principle. It is not cast, like provisions of the Constitution, in general terms. Justice Rehnquist seemed to imply the contrary, that it ought to be and should be judged by such a standard. He suggested that one would expect to find the elements of the trimester framework in the text of the Constitution. He created that expectation and criticized the rule for resembling a code of regulations, which it does, rather than a constitutional principle, which it is not, but which it is meant to serve.*

Recognizing that the Chief Justice was challenging the trimester rule as if it were a constitutional principle and not a means designed to balance various constitutional interests, Justice Blackmun, in dissent, answered:

> With respect to the *Roe* framework, the general constitutional principle,... for which it was developed is the right to privacy,...a species of "liberty" protected by the Due Process Clause, which under our past decisions safeguards the right of women to exercise some control over their own role in procreation....It is this general principle...that is found in the Constitution. The trimester

---

*This observation should not be read to relieve the Court of its obligation to write the rules, the means, that it fashions in an intelligible manner. Recognition of this obligation may underlie Chief Justice Rehnquist's challenge to the *Roe* framework as if it were a constitutional principle.

framework simply defines and limits that right to privacy
in the abortion context to accommodate, not destroy, a
State's legitimate interest in protecting the health of pregnant women and in preserving potential human life. Fashioning such accommodations between individual rights
and the legitimate interests of government, establishing
benchmarks and standards with which to evaluate the
competing claims of individuals and government, lies at
the very heart of constitutional adjudication. To the extent
that the trimester framework is useful in this enterprise,
it is not only consistent with constitutional interpretation,
but necessary to the wise and just exercise of this Court's
paramount authority to define the scope of constitutional
rights.[34]

   Justice Blackmun, like Justice Marshall in *Mc-
Culloch* it would seem, drew a distinction, blurred by
Justice Rehnquist, yet essential to analyzing and understanding opinions as communications expounding the Constitution. That such distinctions are not
always easy to make and that they can be too easily
lost or ignored only highlights the need to recognize
but not oversimplify the basic differences between
means and constitutional principles or provisions in
fulfilling the opinion-writing task when expounding
the Constitution.
   In conflating means and principle and in other
ways that are examined in the chapters that follow,
the justices risk converting the Constitution from
something sufficiently free of detail to be "embraced
by the human mind" to something hardly under-

standable by the general public.[35] Especially in its exposition of individual rights as restraints or obligations on both the federal and state governments, the Court may be gradually altering the character of the Constitution by turning it into a complex body of rules and regulations—into an "instrument for dialectic subtleties."[36]

We the People of the United States under this "increasingly particularistic Constitution" are thus forced to turn more and more to specialists, to experts in constitutional law, in order to gain some understanding of the structure of government and of our fundamental rights as individuals and as members of a group.[37] Even the professional interpreters to whom We turn may not be able to unravel what the Court has to say, often at great length in heavily footnoted multiple opinions reaching not only opposite but even the same results.[38] They, not to mention the justices themselves, may not be able to identify the constitutional principles underlying a decision like *Webster*, for example, whose six opinions and seventy- four pages are introduced with:

> REHNQUIST, C.J., announced the judgment of the Court and delivered the opinion for a unanimous Court with respect to Part II-C, the opinion of the Court with respect to Parts I, II-A, and II-B, in which WHITE, O'CONNOR, SCALIA, and KENNEDY, JJ., joined, and an opinion with respect to Parts II-D and III, in which WHITE and KENNEDY, JJ., joined. O'CONNOR, J.,...and SCALIA, J.,...filed opinions concurring in part and concurring in the judg-

ment. BLACKMUN, J., filed an opinion concurring in part and dissenting in part, in which BRENNAN and MARSHALL, JJ., joined. . . . STEVENS, J., filed an opinion concurring in part and dissenting in part. . . .[39]

Such untoward developments may be as attributable to the opinions of the strict constructionists—the originalists or interpretivists—as they are to those of the noninterpretivists. They may be as attributable to the opinions of a Court that sits as a "superlegislature to weigh the wisdom of legislation"[40] as they are to the opinions of a Court that has "returned to the original constitutional proposition that courts do not substitute their social and economic beliefs for the judgment of legislative bodies."[41]

This book is not concerned with whether the justices find or make law.[42] Indeed, it assumes that law-finding and law-making are never fully separable. Nor is the concern that "judicial decisions," as Ronald Dworkin has insisted, "should be generated by principles, not policy."[43] Rather, the concern is that policy must not determine result unless it can be and is explained in terms of constitutional provisions or principles. Benjamin Cardozo observed: "The great generalities of the constitution have a content and a significance that vary from age to age. The method of free decision sees through the transitory particulars and reaches what is permanent behind them."[44] What is "permanent" behind a decision is the constitutional principle or provision upon which the Court rests its judgment and fashions its rules and remedies.[45] The

court-fashioned "trimester framework," like most statutes and regulations, may be no more than a "transitory
particular." What is "permanent" behind it, though not
static in content, is an individual's constitutional right
of privacy and the state's competing interests in guard-
ing the health and well-being of its people.

V

Whatever the expounding bias of a justice or of the
Court may be, the thesis of this book is that the justices,
as members of a collective body, have an obligation to
maintain the Constitution, in opinions of the Court and
also in concurring and dissenting opinions, as something intelligible—something that We the People of the
United States can understand. Whether the justices be
activists or passivists, they have a professional obligation to articulate in comprehensible and accessible
language the constitutional principles on which their
judgments rest. The Court's goal is to render opinions,
whether or not based on original understanding, that
contemporary society can understand—opinions in
which the principles formulated are linked in an intelligible manner to the Constitution as amended.

That the Constitution be intelligible and accessible
to We the People of the United States is requisite to a
government by consent; a government that guarantees
equal protection and due process of law; a government

that provides both the governed and the governors with a peaceful process for resolving conflicts about the Constitution's meaning, particularly with regard to individual rights. To make this observation is to recognize that the principles the Court develops, like the provisions of the Constitution, will always need interpretation. This is so because of the nature of words and because justices of the Court are no more capable than were the Framers at the Constitutional Convention of foreseeing future exigencies—particularly in settings in which one constitutional principle may come into conflict with another. There is no expectation that the Court's formulations will ever be fully comprehensible or ambiguity-free. But the goal must be that the Court's interpretations of the Constitution are understandable at their core—that they serve to prevent it from taking on the complexity of a body of regulations.[46]

In the examination of the opinions that follow, a search is made for clues that might lead to a more explicit guide to constitutional law-making by the Court than the mere admonition that the justices never forget that it is *a constitution*—indeed, THE CONSTITUTION—they are expounding.

PART II

OPINION STUDIES

The four chapters in this part examine some important constitutional law cases. The purpose is to provide a basis for assessing the adequacy of judicial opinions as communications about the Constitution. The emphasis is not on result but rather on communicative style. The focus is on the extent to which an opinion—whether unanimous, majority, concurring, or dissenting—is a coherent communication about the Constitution.

On the basis of these opinion studies, I suggest in Part III, for the Court's consideration, canons of comprehensibility and a process for making them operational in the opinion-writing enterprise. The suggestions are meant to inform the role of the justices who seek to define and to fulfill their individual and collective obligation "never [to] forget, that it is a constitution [they] are expounding."

CHAPTER 2

WITH STUDIED AMBIGUITY
National League of Cities v. Usery
and
Garcia v. San Antonio Metro
Transit Authority

In 1976, the Supreme Court, in *National League of Cities*, addressed, as it had in *McCulloch* and many times since, the meaning and application of the constitutional principle of federalism.[1] It considered whether the powers "reserved to the States" in the Tenth Amendment place judicially expoundable limitations upon an otherwise proper exercise by Congress of the commerce power.[2] Or, put differently, the Court had to decide whether the federal structure of government provided by the Constitution leaves the imposition of constraints in the name of state sovereignty solely to the political process.

The specific question posed in *National League of Cities* was whether the Constitution empowers Congress to regulate the minimum wages and maximum hours of state employees. Eight years earlier, the Court in *Maryland v. Wirtz* gave an affirmative answer with respect to employees of state hospitals and public schools.[3] *National League of Cities* overruled *Wirtz*. It invalidated federal wage and hour regulations imposed on policemen and firemen.[4] The Court declared that police and fire protection are attributes of state sovereignty that, under the Tenth Amendment, Congress cannot impair.[5] It held that the Commerce Clause does not empower Congress to "directly displace the States' freedom to structure integral operations *in areas of traditional governmental functions.*"[6]

Unlike the *McCulloch* Court, the Court in *National League of Cities* was sharply divided. Justice Brennan wrote a scathing dissent that was joined by Justices White and Marshall. Justice Stevens dissented separately. Justice Rehnquist, joined by Chief Justice Burger and Justices Powell and Stewart, with Justice Blackmun joining in a separate concurrence, wrote what was called the "opinion of the Court."

I

Justice Blackmun's crucial opinion of only a single paragraph prompts asking whether the justices fulfilled their institutional responsibility for ensuring that the label "opinion of the Court" means what it communicates. Since the Rehnquist opinion would *not* have been the Court's opinion without the Blackmun concurrence, the two opinions must be read together in order to determine whether a majority of the justices were in agreement about the constitutional principles on which the Court's judgment rested. The purpose of focusing on the language of Justice Blackmun's opinion is *not* to examine the great constitutional issues concerning state sovereignty and the role of the judicial branch, as opposed to the political branches, in determining the ambit of federalism. Rather, it is to assess the "opinion of the Court" as a communication about the Constitution.

Justice Blackmun, concurring, wrote in entirety:

The Court's opinion and the dissents indicate the importance and significance of this litigation as it bears upon the relationship between the Federal Government and our States. Although *I am not untroubled* by certain possible implications of the Court's opinion—some of them suggested by the dissents—*I do not read the opinion so despairingly* as does my Brother BRENNAN. In my view, *the result* with respect to the statute under challenge here *is* necessarily *correct. I may misinterpret the Court's opinion,* but it seems to me that *it adopts a balancing approach,* and does not outlaw federal power in areas such as environmental protection, where the federal interest is demonstrably greater and where state facility compliance with imposed federal standards would be essential. With this *understanding on my part* of the Court's opinion, *I join it.*[7]

What do these words of the "not untroubled" Justice convey about the institutional obligations of each justice in fulfilling the opinion-making, as opposed to decision-making, task of the Court?

It is not surprising that Justice Blackmun may have been troubled about the opinion he joined. The Brennan dissenters and Justice Stevens alerted him to some of the problems of communication that he had to resolve before casting the vote that created the "opinion of the Court." They could not find in the Rehnquist opinion the constitutional principle on which the holding rested.[8] They could not "identify a [principled] limitation on...federal power that would not also invalidate [permissible] federal regulation of state activities."[9] Indeed, they could not "recall another instance in the Court's history when the reasoning of so many decisions covering so long a span of time has been discarded in such a roughshod manner...[rendering the] decision an *ipse dixit* reflecting nothing but displeasure with a congressional judgment."[10] Justice Blackmun, at the start of his concurrence, observed that he was "not untroubled by [these] implications of the Court's opinion."[11] But he added, "I do not read the opinion so despairingly as does my Brother BRENNAN."[12]

What is significant, however, for purposes of assessing the adequacy of the Court's opinion as a communication about the meaning of the Constitution is not only that Justice Blackmun was unsure that the opinion meant what Justice Brennan read it to say. It is also that Justice Blackmun was not sure of his own reading. "I may," he said, "misinterpret the Court's opinion, but it seems to me that it adopts a balancing approach...."[13] He explicitly rested his pivotal vote on "with this understanding on my part of the Court's opinion, I join it."[14]

Whether the Rehnquist four shared Justice Blackmun's "understanding" was left in doubt. Justice Rehnquist did not unmistakably accept or reject balancing. Rather, he was willing to leave his opinion sufficiently ambiguous to get Justice Blackmun's vote. Justice Blackmun was apparently willing to accept the ambiguity, possibly because he believed, as he said, that the result was "necessarily correct." "One is forced to conclude [that the opinion in *National League of Cities*] is written," as Henry Hart said of the opinion in *Irvin v. Dowd*, "with studied ambiguity ... with a willingness to muddy the waters."[15]

Both Justices seemed to have forgotten that their—the Court's—task is to expound the Constitution so that they and others can have a common understanding of what the Court has said the Constitution means. Justice Blackmun should not have left himself and We the People wondering whether he had "misinterpret[ed]" the opinion that he had joined. Nor should Justice Rehnquist have left Justice Blackmun or We the People wondering. He should have considered himself obligated to confirm or deny the Blackmun "understanding." He should have done more than merely declare, as he did on behalf of the Court, the importance of it being "clear what we hold today, and what we do not."[16]

Both Justices failed to subordinate their individual wishes to their institutional responsibility. Apparently they were unwilling to risk the possibility that their views, if clarified, might not command a majority. The justices who joined the opinion of the Court, as well as those who did not, ought to have been able to comprehend the "meaning" of the Constitution on which a majority of the Court reached its judgment.

II

The justices should have postponed publication of the decision in *National League of Cities* until their opinions left no doubt either that at least five of them shared an interpretation of the Constitution on which their decision was based or that a majority could not find common constitutional ground for the Court's judgment.[17] In furtherance of this shared institutional objective, Justice Blackmun might have written Justice Rehnquist:

Dear Bill,
I agree with the result you reach. It is necessarily correct.
I am troubled, however, by some of the implications

of your opinion. I read it despairingly, albeit not so despairingly as does Bill Brennan. My concern, my question, is simply this: Will a congressional regulation that indisputably crosses the boundary of state sovereignty into "areas of traditional [state] governmental functions"—the line that you draw in your opinion—be unconstitutional, beyond the power of Congress under the Commerce Clause, even if the national interest is greater than the state interest, and even if compliance with the federal standard is deemed essential?

I may misinterpret your opinion, but I think it requires balancing national and state interests in cases involving traditional state and local government functions. I base my belief primarily on your reference to some language from *Fry v. United States*.[18] But I remain uncertain and uneasy about my reading of the language you introduce from *Fry*. It is not essential to the holding in the case, nor do you use it to suggest that balancing has a place in your constitutional rule. My doubt about my relying on your use of *Fry* stems as well from the fact that the holding in that case depended primarily on *Wirtz*, which you understandably would overrule.[19] Indeed, I am sure that you will recall saying in your *Fry* dissent: "The Court's opinion . . . not unreasonably relies on *Wirtz* in holding that Congress may impose across-the-board limitations on salary increases for all state employees."[20]

If my reading of your position on balancing is correct, and I hope it is, I will join your opinion to make it the opinion of the Court. But before I do, I hope that if you share my reading, you will make it explicit in your opinion. In that event, I will not write a separate concurrence.

Even if we agree on words about the meaning and place of balancing in the "traditional governmental function" test that you propose, we must recognize that the courts below are likely to encounter difficulties in applying it. We must assume that only a case-by-case development will lead the Court to a workable, comprehensible standard for determining whether a particular governmental function should be immune from federal regulation under the Commerce Clause.[21]

If, however, I do misinterpret your constitutional view, I must, of course, write separately. I would, I believe, still concur in your judgment. But I would explain why I cannot join your opinion. Accordingly, and unfortunately, there will be no opinion of the Court, only a plurality decision. Though it would seem incongruous, *Wirtz* then would, I suppose, remain standing.

Undesirable as plurality opinions may be, they are better than opinions of the Court that mislead, that cause confusion where clarity is sought, and that have a majority in name only. Such conscious failures of communication disserve our institutional obligations to maintain the Constitution as something intelligible, especially with regard to a matter so significant as the relationship between the federal government and the states.

One more matter contributes in a small way to my sense of despair, particularly if the resolution of my concerns were to require my joining only in the judgment. A concurrence, though I "feel" certain that the result you reach is correct, would leave the Court unnecessarily vulnerable to Bill Brennan's charge that it expresses "nothing but displeasure with a congressional judgment." I know that were I a member of Congress, and not an Article III court judge,* I would have voted against the extension of wage and hour regulations to the states as employers. If we cannot provide an understandable balancing approach that validates the exercise of federal power in areas where the national interest is greater than the state interest, perhaps I should join John Stevens, who writes in his dissent:

> My disagreement with the wisdom of this legislation may not, of course, affect my judgment with respect to its validity.... Since I am unable to identify a limitation on that federal power that would not also invalidate federal regulation of state activities that I consider unquestionably permissible, I am persuaded that this statute is valid. Accordingly, with respect and a great deal of sympathy for the views expressed by the Court, I dissent from its constitutional holding.[22]

In trying to come to terms with my despair and in trying to think through how best to satisfy our institu-

---

*U.S. Const. art. III, § 1 reads: "The judicial Power of the United States, shall be vested in one supreme Court, and in such inferior Courts as the Congress may from time to time ordain and establish. The Judges, both of the supreme and inferior Courts, shall hold their Offices during good Behaviour, and shall, at stated Times, receive for their Services a Compensation, which shall not be diminished during their Continuance in Office."

tional obligations, I was reminded of Justice Frankfurter's observation that "[t]he Court should not rest on the first attempt at explanation for what sound instinct counsels. It should not forgo re-examination to clarity of thought, because confused and inadequate analysis is too apt gradually to lead from the true ends to be pursued."[23]

Together we must find (or acknowledge that we cannot find) comprehensible language for a principled standard that identifies state activities that are exempt from congressional regulation under the Commerce Clause.

Harry

And in a Court whose members are driven or restrained by a true expounder's sense of institutional pride in the Court's communications about the Constitution, Justice Rehnquist, on receipt of Justice Blackmun's proposed concurrence, might have visited his chambers or phoned him to say:

Your concurrence makes me wonder whether you mean to cast your vote for my opinion. The language of my opinion neither provides for nor anticipates the use of "balancing" in my test.

It reads the Tenth Amendment to mean that Congress cannot act under its commerce power to "displace the States' freedom to structure [their own] operations in areas of traditional governmental functions."[24]

The understanding on your part with which you intend to join me is mistaken.

Apparently there were no such exchanges. Justice Blackmun officially joined the Rehnquist opinion to make it the opinion of the Court. At the same time, in his separate opinion, he took distance from the constitutional position of the Court majority that he had created. His explicit admission that he may have misunderstood the opinion he joined should have alerted every member of the Court to the need for clarification before publication.

The members of the Court, it would seem, forgot that their task was to maintain the Constitution as something comprehensible to the People. They failed to insist that removable doubts about the meaning of the Court's opinion be eliminated before releasing it. Such malfunctions in the process of collective opinion-making can only cause confusion where coherence must be the goal.

We the People and Justice Blackmun should not have been left wondering whether he "misinterpret[ed]" the opinion that he joined. Justice Rehnquist should have been obligated to confirm or deny the Blackmun "understanding." He should have been willing to risk the possibility that Brennan's opinion (joined by Blackmun) would become the opinion of the Court and that his own opinion would become a dissent. He should have acknowledged, as he disclosed nine years later in a one-paragraph dissent in *Garcia v. San Antonio Metro Transit Authority*, that his "opinion of the Court" did not provide for balancing.[25]

III

In *Garcia*, the Court overruled *National League of Cities* by a 5 to 4 vote. Justice Blackmun, for an unsplintered majority, wrote the opinion of the Court. Of the three dissenting opinions, only that of Justice Powell spoke for the fragmented minority of four. The Blackmun and Powell opinions are cogent, coherent, thoughtful, and carefully crafted communications that take different positions with respect to the constitutionality of the imposition by Congress of wage and hour regulations on states as employers. Though only the opinion of the Court is controlling, both opinions provide a basis for understanding and possibly reconciling "the Constitution's dual concerns for federalism and an effective commerce power."[26] "[I]t does not seem surprising," as Andrew Kaufman has observed, that "the Court should have ended up closely divided. ... [I]n a constitutional sense both positions were reasonable and...there was not one clearly 'right' answer."[27] These opinions, each a "persuasive" communication, served to clarify what the Court did and did not decide and why it has had difficulty in determining with any finality whether the federal system has, in the words of Charles Black, "any core of constitutional right that courts will enforce."[28]

On one issue, the importance of taking seriously the principle of *stare decisis*, the entire Court seemed to be in agreement. "*Stare decisis et non quieta movere*" instructs courts to "stand by the precedents and do not disturb the calm."[29] For the Court, Justice Blackmun observed, "We do not lightly overrule recent precedent."[30] Justice Powell, for all of the dissenters, wrote: "Although the doctrine is not rigidly applied to constitutional questions, 'any departure from the doctrine of *stare decisis* demands special justification.' "[31]

The Blackmun opinion takes *stare decisis* seriously and meets the demands of "special justification." Only after canvassing eight years of lower court experience applying the *National League of Cities* rule and only after reviewing the words of the Framers and of the Court on federalism did the majority decide to "reject, as unsound in principle and unworkable in practice, a rule of state immunity from federal regulation."[32] The district court in *Garcia* had observed, "If [state] transit is to be distinguished from the exempt [*National League of Cities*] functions it will have to be by identifying a traditional state function in the same way pornography is sometimes identified: someone knows it when they see it, but they can't describe it."[33] Recognizing the plight confronting the lower courts and administrative agencies, the Court concluded that any such rule "disserves principles of democratic self-governance, and it breeds inconsistency precisely because it is divorced from these principles."[34] In other words, it is ruleless.

No matter how reasonable the dissenters' contrary interpretation of constitutional history and court experience may be, it does not provide a basis for charging, as they did, that the Court "ignored" the principle of *stare decisis* and that its decision to overrule was "precipitate."[35] These unwarranted charges surround the doctrine of *stare decisis* with confusion and cast doubt on the genuineness of the dissenters' express interest in strengthening its application in the service of the "stability of judicial decision, and ... the authority of this Court."[36] The opinions of Justices Rehnquist and O'Connor reinforce the doubt and add to the confusion.

On the issue of *stare decisis*, Justice Rehnquist in his dissent distanced himself from the Powell opinion that he joined. He simply said: " ... I do not think it incumbent on those of us in dissent to spell out ... the fine points of a [constitutional] principle that will, I am confident, in time again command the support of a majority of this Court."[37]

Likewise on *stare decisis*, Justice O'Connor distanced herself from the Powell opinion that she joined by closing her dissent with these words:

> [W]henever constitutional concerns as important as federalism and the effectiveness of the commerce power come into conflict ... it is and will remain the duty of this Court [and not the duty of the political process alone as this Court decides today] to reconcile these concerns in the final instance.... I would not shirk the duty acknowl-

edged by *National League of Cities* ... [even though the Court now overrules it]. I share JUSTICE REHNQUIST's belief that this Court will in time again assume its constitutional responsibility.[38]

The words I have added in brackets make obvious, but do not alter, the meaning for *stare decisis* of Justice O'Connor's statement. Finally, on *stare decisis*, by joining Justice O'Connor's dissent and, by implication, that of Justice Rehnquist, Justice Powell distanced himself from his own opinion. Thus Justices Powell, Rehnquist, and O'Connor threaten to undermine the doctrine of *stare decisis* while appearing to support it. What they seem to be saying is, "We do not intend to abide by the opinion of the Court."

Rather than charge the Court with ignoring *stare decisis*, the dissenters, had they meant what was said in Justice Powell's opinion about protecting the stability of judicial decisions and the authority of the Court, might have urged him to write instead:

I said in *Mitchell v. W. T. Grant Co.* with respect to *stare decisis*: "It is ... not only our prerogative but also our duty to re-examine a precedent where its reasoning or understanding of the Constitution is fairly called into question. And if the precedent or its rationale is of doubtful validity, then it should not stand."[39] The entire Court has taken seriously, in accord with the principle of *stare decisis*, what we decided in *National League of Cities* and its progeny. Though we dissent, we rec-

ognize that the Court has fulfilled its duty and interpreted the Constitution in a comprehensible and
carefully crafted opinion. Thus the Court's opinion, with
which we disagree, is entitled to the precedential value
associated with the principle of *stare decisis*.

More than time must pass if *Garcia* is to be overruled. It is to be followed unless and until experience
teaches us that it disserves the constitutional principle
of federalism or that a principled rule can be fashioned
for better safeguarding state sovereignty without in-
truding on the commerce power. Today we overrule
National League of Cities and reaffirm *Maryland v.
Wirtz*, which *National League of Cities* overruled.
What the Court decides today, however you view this
past, deserves the weight of precedent and deserves to
be followed in good faith—not just until another vote
can be found.

The justices, in their institutional role, must ensure that
the Court's communications concerning the doctrine
of *stare decisis* are "not used to breed the uncertainty
which it is supposed to dispel."[40]

Opinion-writing must become a process of inform-
ing for a vote. It must be a process of clarification
characterized by candor. It must not be a process of
obfuscation characterized by disingenuousness. The
votes that justices get or are denied, the votes that they
give or refuse, should be based on a shared understand-

ing of what an opinion means, not just on the bottom line, not just on the result. To vote otherwise can only lead the justices, individually and collectively, to forget We the People for whom and to whom they are expounding the Constitution.

CHAPTER 3

HAD UNDERSTANDING BEEN THE GOAL

Cooper v. Aaron

Another illustration of ambiguity infecting the work of the Court is to be found in its unanimous and apparently uncompromising opinion in *Cooper v. Aaron*.[1] Here ambiguity was not employed, as in *National League of Cities*, to win the vote of a colleague. Rather it was used, as can be learned only by going outside the opinion, to win acceptance or at least to avoid further resistance from We the white People of Little Rock, Arkansas, who, encouraged and aided by state officials, had forcibly prevented the Little Rock School Board from carrying out its court-approved plan for a step-by-step elimination of racial segregation in its schools.

After hearing the case in a special session in August 1958, the Supreme Court affirmed a court of appeals

judgment to enforce what the Supreme Court described
as the "plan for desegregation in compliance with the
decision of this Court in *Brown v. Board of Education*,"
which had declared racially segregated schools unconstitutional.[2] By a 2 to 1 vote, the court of appeals had
reversed a district court's decision to suspend what
both courts had described as the "plan of integration"
for the public schools of Little Rock.[3]

In an environment of "extreme public hostility
engendered largely by the official attitude and actions
of the Governor and the Legislature," the school board
had concluded that it could not meet its educational
responsibilities.* It had sought and obtained from the
district court "permission to suspend the operation of
the plan of integration."[4] The court of appeals had said
that "the precise question at issue ... [was] whether a
plan of integration, once in operation, may lawfully be
suspended because of popular opposition ... mani-
fested in overt acts of violence."[5] It had held that "overt
public resistance, including mob protest, [did not con-
stitute] ... sufficient cause to nullify an order of the federal court directing the Board to proceed with its
integration plan."[6] In other words, no state interest,
including the prevention of violence threatened, was

*"In its petition for certiorari filed in this Court, the School Board
itself describes the situation in this language: 'The legislative, executive, and
judicial departments of the state government opposed the desegregation of
Little Rock schools by enacting laws, calling out troops, making statements
vilifying federal law and federal courts, and failing to utilize state law enforcement agencies and judicial processes to maintain public peace.'"
Cooper v. Aaron, 358 U.S. 1, 15 (1958).

compelling enough to justify further postponement of a plan designed to end gradually the violation of the constitutional rights of public-school children in Little Rock. *"We say the time has not yet come in these United States when an order of a Federal Court must be whittled away, watered down, or shamefully withdrawn in the face of violent and unlawful acts of individual citizens in opposition thereto."*[7]

Because of the tense atmosphere and because the new school year was about to start, the Supreme Court promptly affirmed the court of appeals decision and reserved to a later date the issuance of an opinion. That opinion, unambiguous on its face, is the subject of the examination that follows.

I

At the start of the Court's full opinion in *Cooper v. Aaron*—signed, as had not been done before and has not been done since, by each justice individually[8]—the Court stressed that the case "raises questions of the highest importance to the maintenance of our federal system of government."[9] The opinion had to respond in no uncertain terms to "a claim by the Governor and Legislature of a State that [they need not]... obey federal court orders resting on the Court's considered interpretation of the United States Constitution."[10] The Court had to remove any doubt from the public mind about the constitutional duty of state authorities under the Equal Protection Clause of the Fourteenth Amendment to bring about "the elimination of racial discrimination in the public school system"[11]—in this case, to implement the approved "Plan of School Integration."[12] Its opinion, in the face of violent opposition, had to make "plain that delay in any guise in order to deny the constitutional rights of Negro children could not be countenanced."[13]

The Court in *Cooper v. Aaron* thus appeared unequivocal in asserting "that the interpretation of the Fourteenth Amendment enunciated by this Court in the *Brown* case is the supreme law of the land, and Art. VI of the Constitution makes it of binding effect on the States 'any Thing in the Constitution or Laws of any State to the Contrary notwithstanding.' "[14] For the Court, the controlling constitutional principles were "plain":

> The command of the Fourteenth Amendment is that no "State" shall deny to any person within its jurisdiction the equal protection of the laws....In short, the constitutional rights of children not to be discriminated against in school admission on grounds of race or color declared by this Court in the *Brown* case can neither be nullified openly and directly by state legislators or state executive or judicial officers, nor nullified indirectly by them through evasive schemes for segregation whether attempted "ingeniously or ingenuously."[15]

With these powerful words, the Court told the people of Arkansas—indeed, of every state of the United

States—and the officials who act for them what the Constitution demands.

Unanimous in its opinion, the Court sought to establish a reality of constitutional order and law in which the state and local authorities were to operate the public schools. It rejected the notion that the constitutional rights of children may be sacrificed to accommodate the reality of violence or the reality of covert schemes designed to deprive them of their rights. Instead, the Court insisted that reality comply "now" with basic constitutional propositions, not that these propositions be fashioned or refashioned to satisfy a reality of open or covert defiance.[16]

Accordingly, the Court closed its opinion with words that would seem to eliminate any doubt not only about the meaning of *Brown* but also about that of the Fourteenth Amendment. "The principles announced in that decision and the obedience of the States to them, according to the command of the Constitution, are indispensable for the protection of the freedoms guaranteed by our fundamental charter for all of us. Our constitutional ideal of equal justice under law is thus made a living truth."[17]

Yet the Court did cast doubt on the meaning of its decision by using throughout its opinion words of "desegregation" instead of words of "integration," which both lower courts had used to describe the Little Rock Plan. By not acknowledging and by not explaining this word change, the Court made ambiguous an opinion that was unambiguous on its face. To discover why the

Court substituted "desegregation" for "integration" and why it chose to do so without explicitly saying what it was doing ought not to require going outside the opinion of the Court. But it does. Without explicitly disclosing what it was doing, the Court did create doubt about the remedy for violations of the "constitutional rights of Negro children" in the public schools. And consequently, it did cast doubt on the meaning of the constitutional right.

II

Justice Brennan, who is understood to have been primarily responsible for drafting the Court's opinion, recalled in a 1987 radio interview that early in September 1958, while sitting on his porch working on *Cooper v. Aaron*, his neighbor Richard Harkness, an NBC reporter, stopped by:

> *Brennan:* I was working on some suggested language on it... and he strolled over and he said to me that you know I have just been on tour through the South and I have discovered that the one buzz word in the South is the word integration. Desegregation is not resented but integration is resented. And that was a word that appeared in the lower court opinions in that case and so I just substituted desegregation wherever I had used the word integration. And I don't think you find the word integration in the opinion now.

Interviewer: Do you think it made a difference?

Brennan: I was just taken with Richard Harkness's suggestion that it made a difference to people in the South and after all we were writing an opinion that we had hoped would find understanding and acceptance in the South as well as everywhere else in the country.[18]*

Did the Court, merely by substituting "desegregation" for "integration," equate the constitutional meaning of the two words? If "desegregation" and "integration" are to be understood as constitutional synonyms, which word is to take on the meaning of the other? Which meaning is to serve as a basis for determining "good faith compliance" with the *Brown* decisions? Which word is to be used in defining what means may be employed to enforce the constitutional right? The Court left these questions unposed and unanswered.

---

*The announcement of the Court's unanimous opinion in *Cooper* was followed seven days later by a concurrence from Justice Frankfurter, even though he had "unreservedly participat[ed] with [his] brethren in [their] joint opinion." *Cooper v. Aaron*, 358 U.S. 1, 20 (1958). In his concurrence, also unambiguous on its face, Justice Frankfurter used neither "integration" nor "desegregation." He noted that the Court decided "in the *Brown* case that the Constitution precludes compulsory segregation based on color in state supported schools." *Id.* at 26. With respect to the constitutional rights of black children, Frankfurter observed that the lower courts had approved "the Board's non-segregation plan." *Id.* He sought primarily to reinforce the proposition that for a state "to defy the law of the land is profoundly subversive not only of our constitutional system but of the presuppositions of a democratic society." *Id.* at 22. He added, "The duty to abstain from resistance to the supreme law of the land...does not require immediate approval of it nor does it deny the right of...dissent. Criticism need not be stilled. Active obstruction or defiance is barred." *Id.* at 24. For a description of the circumstances under which the concurrence was released, see Chapter 6.

Justice Brennan's interview indicates, however, that he believed that these words did not mean the same thing, at least to We the white People of the South. "Integration" seemed to carry with it the affirmative obligation to "mix" whites and blacks in the public schools, to break down the social barriers to nonsegregated schools. "Desegregation" seemed to mean no more than the removal of legal barriers to nonsegregated schools. Integration and desegregation had been sharply distinguished in *Briggs v. Elliott* by the three-judge district court to which the *Brown* Court had remanded the case in 1955 for orders of compliance. Judge John J. Parker, construing the *Brown* decision in *Briggs*, wrote:*

> [I]t is important that we point out exactly what the Supreme Court has decided and what it has not decided in this case.... It has not decided that the states must mix persons of different races in the schools.... What it has decided, and all that it has decided, is that a state may not deny to any person on account of race the right to attend any school that it maintains.... Nothing in the Constitution or in the decision of the Supreme Court takes away from the people freedom to choose the schools they attend. *The Constitution ... does not require integration.* It merely forbids discrimination. It does not forbid such segregation as occurs as the result of voluntary action. It merely forbids the use of governmental power to enforce segregation.[19]

*For studies of the *Brown v. Board of Education* opinions, see Chapter 4.

There is no doubt that the language of integration and the language of desegregation sent significantly different messages, or at least were intended to do so. The so-called Parker doctrine, Richard Kluger wrote in *Simple Justice,* "was widely seized upon by Southern courts to approve a variety of maneuvers designed to deflect the impact of *Brown* in those states and school districts that did not turn to outright defiance of the Court."[20] Yet in *Cooper,* the Court did not acknowledge that "integration" was the operative word in the lower court's order, let alone disclose that it chose to use "desegregation" instead and explain why.

If the Court thought it important enough to delete the language of integration from an opinion vigorously affirming a lower court decision to enforce a plan of integration, it would seem to be equally important for the Court to explain why it chose to do so. Since the court of appeals in *Cooper* had commended the school board for having "moved promptly [following the first *Brown* decision] to promulgate a plan designed to gradually bring about complete integration in the Little Rock public schools,"[21] the Supreme Court was especially obligated to disclose why it dropped all words of integration in its opinion justifying its decision to affirm an order of integration. The court of appeals had used the language of integration twenty-seven times and the word "desegregation" only twice in its opinion. But the Supreme Court failed to explain why it blurred the message it was sending to the resisters. It thus disserved its professed goal of speaking loud and clear not only to the recalcitrant but also to all school children and their parents, white and black, about their constitutional rights. As a result, the Court failed in its obligation to enable We the People—both black and white—to better understand the meaning of the Fourteenth Amendment as it applied to public education. To minimize white resistance—to "buy peace" from a powerful majority—the Court promoted confusion rather than understanding.

III

If understanding had been the goal—as it should have been and as Justice Brennan declared it was—the Court would have explained why the language of desegregation replaced the language of integration. It might, for example, have adopted Judge Parker's interpretation of what the Court had decided in *Brown* and said:

The Constitution requires no more than desegregation— no more than the removal of state-enforced racial barriers—in order to remedy the violations of the constitutional rights of the school children.

Or the Court might have modified Judge Parker's reading and said:

Though we recognize the crucial distinction between "Thou Shalt Not Segregate" and "Thou Shalt Integrate," we are persuaded that the language of desegregation correctly conveys the Court's current understanding of the means authorized for implementing the Equal Protection Clause. Desegregation is sufficiently open-textured to allow the Court, if case and controversy dictate, to order integration as a remedy. The word "desegregation," not "integration," best describes the Little Rock School Board's plan that the court of appeals reinstated. The gradual, step-by-step elimination of *legal* barriers is its essential characteristic. Ultimately with its implementation may come the gradual elimination of the *social* barriers that support these dual systems of public education.

Minimally, the Court should have seen itself as obligated to acknowledge that it was aware of the difference between the language of its opinion and that of the court of appeals decision that it affirmed. It should have acknowledged that to affirm the Little Rock Plan—even with its integration title—required no more from the Court than the use of the less concrete language of desegregation. Whatever word the Court decided to use, it had an obligation to clarify its Equal Protection meaning.

Instead, what the Court did was to play prophet and politician—roles that it was neither competent nor qualified to assume.[22] It attempted—as Justice Bren-

nan's interview and not his opinion reveals—to defuse
the resistance of those in power with a "euphemistic"
reading of the Constitution, or, put another way, to risk
the outrage of the less rather than the more powerful.

Justice Brennan "hoped" to write an opinion that
"would find understanding and acceptance in the
South." But the opinion could only have led to acceptance through misunderstanding. However, acceptance
was not to be. On the day that the Supreme Court
entered its desegregation order in *Cooper v. Aaron*,
Governor Faubus issued a proclamation closing all the
senior high schools in Little Rock. He ignored the
Court's desegregation language and called for a vote
on the proposition that "no school within the district
shall be integrated" and that a school closed by executive order "shall remain closed until such executive
order is countermanded by proclamation of the Governor."[23] By a large margin, the vote was against racial
integration.[24] Even if Governor Faubus had used the
word "desegregation" and even if the voters had approved the Little Rock Plan, the Court's failure to explain how the Equal Protection Clause was to be
understood would not have been justified.

The opinion of the Court, read without the opinion
of the court of appeals, would suggest that there must
be no room for misunderstanding by the resisters. It
intended to make "plain" to We the black and white
People of the United States that "delay in any guise in
order to deny the constitutional rights of Negro children could not be countenanced [and that] State au-

thorities were thus duty bound to devote every effort toward . . . bringing about the elimination of racial discrimination in the public school system."[25] Yet, at the same time, the Court was sending, or at least thought it was sending, a covert message to all concerned, black and white, that the opinion neither meant quite what it said nor said what it meant. But the circumstances called for candor, not for ambivalent ambiguity, for "descriptive scrupulousness," not for euphemism.[26] By not being meticulous and by not explaining its choice of words, the Court in *Cooper v. Aaron* failed in its obligation to maintain the Constitution as an instrument accessible and intelligible to We the People. It failed to enhance Our understanding of the meaning of equal protection for public schools, not just in Little Rock, but everywhere.

CHAPTER 4

DECISIONS UNEXPLAINED
The *Brown v. Board of Education* Cases

The Court's failure to communicate the constitutional requisites for relief from school segregation in *Cooper v. Aaron* may be but a reflection of the confusion that characterized its handling of the remedy question in the *Brown v. Board of Education* cases.[1] In *Brown I*, the Court unequivocally established the principle that the use of race as the basis for the assignment of students in the public schools violates the Equal Protection Clause of the Fourteenth Amendment. It determined that the constitutional guarantee of equal protection of the laws could no longer be satisfied—as it could have been until then under *Plessy v. Ferguson*—by separate and equal schools.[2] "Separate educational facilities," the Court said, "are inherently unequal."[3] It held that the plaintiffs—Oliver Brown of Topeka, Kansas; Harry Briggs, Jr., of Clarendon, South

Carolina; Dorothy C. Davis of Prince Edward County,
Virginia; Ethel Louise Belton of New Castle County,
Delaware—and others similarly segregated "for whom
the actions have been brought" were being "deprived
of the equal protection of the laws guaranteed by the
Fourteenth Amendment."[4] On the same day, the Court
held that the segregation in the District of Columbia
public schools of Spottswood Thomas Bolling and
other named students because of their race "is a denial
of the due process of law guaranteed by the Fifth
Amendment to the Constitution."[5]

I

In a memorandum to members of the Court dated May
7, 1954, Chief Justice Warren urged with regard to these
cases that "the opinions should be short, readable by
the lay public, non-rhetorical, unemotional and, above
all, non-accusatory."[6] As communications, these unanimous opinions totaling only fourteen pages appear to
meet the Chief Justice's requirements. But are they in
fact comprehensible to We the People, the lay public,
or even the law-trained?

Only the Kansas schools had been found by a lower
court to have satisfied both prongs of *Plessy*, the then-
prevailing constitutional standard—separate and equal.
In South Carolina, Virginia, and Delaware, the courts
had held that the states were violating the then-

recognized equal protection right of the black children
to separate and equal facilities.[7] They found the black
schools to be "inferior" to white schools with respect to,
for example, buildings, curricula, and transportation. In
Bolling, the District of Columbia plaintiffs did not raise
the question of noncompliance with the *Plessy* requisites, which applied to state, as opposed to federal, action. But they knew that their schools were "plainly
inferior"—separate and unequal. Their suit followed the
Board of Education's refusal to admit them to John
Philip Sousa Junior High School, "a spacious glass-and-
brick structure...in a solidly residential section...
[with] forty-two bright classrooms, a 600-seat audito-
rium,...a double gymnasium, a playground with seven
basketball courts, a softball field, and no Negroes."[8]
Young Bolling attended Shaw Junior High, "forty-eight
years old, dingy, ill-equipped...[with a] science labo-
ratory consist[ing] of one Bunsen burner and a bowl
of goldfish."[9]

Given these circumstances and the Court's exposition of the Constitution in *Brown I* and *Bolling*, how
could Oliver Brown, Harry Briggs, Jr., Dorothy Davis,
Ethel Louise Belton, and Spottswood Bolling—for that
matter anyone, including their parents and their school
boards—have understood the Constitution to mean
anything less than that these children could no longer
be compelled to attend segregated public schools?[10]
Yet the Court in the last paragraph of these opinions
postponed granting—indeed, indefinitely denied to
these children—the right to attend nonsegregated pub-

lic schools.[11] Instead, the Court, having "now announced that such segregation is a denial of the equal protection of the laws,"[12] ordered a reargument on whether its decisions required "that, within the limits set by normal geographic school districting, Negro children should forthwith be admitted to schools of their choice, or ... [whether] this Court [may], in the exercise of its equity powers, permit an effective gradual adjustment to be brought about from existing segregated systems to a system not based on color distinctions."[13]

These were not new questions. They were the last two of five questions that the Court originally propounded at the close of its 1952 term, after deciding to defer judgment in *Brown I* and *Bolling* and to order reargument in the 1953 term. Though the parties had addressed the questions, the Court, transposing its holdings into the "announcement," postponed its answers "because of the wide applicability" of its decisions and because the "variety of local conditions" presented "problems of considerable complexity" in the formulation of decrees.[14] Thus it invited the "Attorneys General of the states requiring or permitting segregation in public education" to file so-called friend-of-the-court briefs and thereby appear as *amici curiae*.[15]

The Court did not reformulate its questions to specifically take into account its holdings that the named plaintiffs and others similarly situated in Topeka, Clarendon, Prince Edward County, and New Castle County were being "deprived of the equal protection of the laws guaranteed by the Fourteenth Amendment"[16] and, in the

District of Columbia, of "the due process of law guaranteed by the Fifth Amendment of the Constitution."[17] Nor did the Court explain to the students directly involved in these controversies the constitutional basis for its authority to permit the continuation of Court-held violations of their constitutional rights. It left unnoted and unaddressed its declaration in *Sweatt v. Painter* and *McLaurin v. Oklahoma State Regents*[18]— cases involving equal-protection violations against graduate and law students—that such rights are "personal and present."[19] It did not explain what could not be understood without explanation: its decision that the constitutional rights of Oliver Brown, Henry Briggs, Jr., Dorothy Davis, Ethel Louise Belton, and all their classmates in the crucial years of their development are less "personal" and less urgently "present" than those of the graduate students Sweatt and McLaurin.*

As for Spottswood Bolling and his classmates, the Court failed to consider whether the violation of their constitutional rights under the Due Process Clause of

---

*In the final round of the reargument that followed *Brown I*, counsel "Spottswood Robinson was...steadfast in pushing the Court for desegregation of the Prince Edward schools in Virginia.... The rights asserted in these cases, Robinson said, were the rights of children 'and if they are ever going to be satisfied, they must be satisfied while they are still children.' The period for attending public schools was a short one, and every delay was an irredeemable one." R. Kluger, *Simple Justice* (1975), 729.

Delay resulting from the Court's order of reargument in 1953—though no less damaging to the children's educational opportunities—did not raise the same issue concerning the Court's authority, since it had not yet held that the constitutional rights of the plaintiff students had been violated. *Brown v. Board of Education*, 347 U.S. 483, 488 (1954).

the Fifth Amendment entitled them to immediate relief or at least to a separate reformulation of the questions for reargument. The Court in *Bolling*, guided by the strict-scrutiny test established in *Korematsu v. United States*, found that the discrimination in the District of Columbia schools, unlike that against Korematsu and other citizens of Japanese origin during World War II where a "[p]ressing public necessity" was said to exist, was not "for a proper governmental objective" and was "a denial of the due process" guaranteed by the Fifth Amendment.[20]* Minimally, the question the Court should have addressed in deciding *Bolling* or in formulating questions for reargument was whether there was or could be a "pressing public necessity" justifying the postponement, or even denial, of relief for constitutional violations resting on a prior finding that no such justification existed.

Without acknowledging the implications of what it was doing, the Court depersonalized, delocalized, and made less than urgent the proven claims of the individual schoolchildren in *Brown* and *Bolling*. It explained that it was calling for a reargument on the "appropriate relief" "because of the wide applicability

---

*The Court declared in *Bolling v. Sharpe*, 347 U.S. 497, 499 (1954), "Classifications based solely upon race must be scrutinized with particular care, since they are contrary to our traditions and hence constitutionally suspect." To support this proposition, it cited *Korematsu v. United States*, 323 U.S. 214 (1944), a case upholding the conviction of a Japanese-American for refusing to abide by a post–Pearl Harbor military regulation prohibiting American citizens of Japanese descent from living or working on the West Coast of the United States.

of this decision, and because of the great variety of local conditions."[21]

II

In *Brown II*, Chief Justice Warren, speaking for the entire Court and noting the "nationwide importance" of the decisions in *Brown I* and *Bolling*, incorporated the two cases "by reference" and read them as precedents "declaring the fundamental principle that racial discrimination in public education is unconstitutional. ... All provisions of federal, state, or local law requiring or permitting such discrimination must yield to this principle."[22] This principle, reflected in the three opinions that now may be treated together as one, appears to be comprehensible and understandable. What was left for the Court to consider in "nationwide" terms was how the phrase "yield to this principle" was to be understood in fashioning the appropriate relief.

With its focus initially on nationwide concerns, as opposed to "the parties to these cases,"[23] the Court answered by implication and without explanation the reargued question 4(a): "[W]ould a decree necessarily follow providing that, within the limits set by normal geographic school districting, Negro children should forthwith be admitted to schools of their choice?"[24] The Court simply observed that the briefs and oral argument were helpful in its consideration of "the complexities

arising from the transition to a system of public education freed of racial discrimination," complexities it
had already used to justify postponement of relief in
order to hear reargument.[25] The Court repeated what
it had initially noted in *Brown I* and *Bolling*, that "implementation of these constitutional principles may require solution of varied local school problems."[26] After
noting that the presentations "demonstrated that substantial steps to eliminate racial discrimination in public schools have already been taken," the Court
concluded that "the courts which originally heard these
cases can best perform this judicial appraisal" on remand.[27] Thus the Court avoided an examination of a
critical question it had posed for reargument.

In reaching its unexplained answer to its "4(a)"
question, the Court answered affirmatively, again without explanation, question 4(b): "[M]ay this Court, in the
exercise of its equity powers, permit an effective gradual adjustment to be brought about from existing segregated systems to a system not based on color
distinctions?"[28] The Court simply asserted, at the start
of the next paragraph of its opinion, that "[i]n fashioning
and effectuating the decrees, the courts will be guided
by equitable principles."[29] It never addressed the may-
this-Court-in-the-exercise-of-its-equity-powers-permit
question. It merely turned to its last question, "5,"
which asked:

[A]ssuming . . . that this Court will exercise its equity powers . . . (a) should this Court formulate detailed decrees in

these cases [already answered NO];...(d) should this Court remand to the courts of first instance with directions to frame decrees in these cases [already answered YES] and if so *what general directions should... the courts of first instance follow in arriving at the specific terms of more detailed decrees?*[30]

Only the italicized question remained. The others were answered by implication and without candor—without the answers ever having been directly justified. Essentially, the Court responded to the issues raised by the questions it had posed without addressing them, and without regard to the actual parties to the controversies.

In *Brown II*, the Court gave its fullest response to the question concerning what general directions it should give to the lower courts for remedying the violations of constitutional rights. It concluded that the courts of first instance should "enter such orders...as are necessary and proper to admit to public schools on a racially nondiscriminatory basis with all deliberate speed the parties to these cases."[31] Before assessing the comprehensibility of the explanation in the *Brown II* opinion for its all-deliberate-speed conclusion, I pause to consider the kinds of questions the Court ought to have fashioned at the close of its *Brown I* and *Bolling* opinions, once it had decided that there should be another hearing on what the remedy should be for the now proven violations of equal protection. It should have substituted for its "general" and "nationwide," delocalized, depersonalized, and detemporalized questions something like the following questions for reargument:

Recognizing that we now hold that the schoolchildren in these cases are being denied their constitutional right not to be segregated by race in the public schools,

(1) may this Court, in the exercise of its equity powers and in accord with the maxim that "[e]quity will not disturb the legal [and constitutional] rights of a party unless his adversary can show some superior equity,"[32] **weigh other than constitutionally-rooted interests against the constitutional right of the schoolchildren** in determining that prompt compliance with the Constitution is not required?

(2) in response to the request of those school systems that are and have been in violation of our "separate and equal" understanding of what the Constitution until this day permitted, may this Court, in exercising its equity powers in accord with the maxim that "he who comes into equity must come with clean hands,"[33] permit the violation of the schoolchildren's personal constitutional rights to continue in order to promote, under our new reading in *Brown*, a gradual adjustment to a system not based on racial distinctions?*

(3) may this Court, in the exercise of its equity powers and in accord with the maxim that "equity will

---

*" 'Unclean hands' includes any unconscionable conduct with relation to the transaction involved in the suit." H. McClintock, *Handbook of the Principles of Equity* (2d ed. 1948), 59–60. "Almost always the violation of any statute will make a party's hands unclean." *Id*. at 62. May anything less be said of a violation of the Constitution?

not suffer a wrong without a remedy,"[34] deny the District of Columbia children prompt admission to the schools of their choice unless the District of Columbia, in accord with our decision in *Korematsu*, on which we rely in *Bolling*, establishes that the "problems of considerable complexity,"[35] which prompt our calling for reargument, constitute a "[p]ressing public necessity" not caused by "racial antagonism"?[36]

But the Court failed (or decided not) to pose such questions. It may have done this to distance itself from the actual cases and controversies before it in order to address "nationwide" interests.[37] Thus the Court in its *Brown II* opinion did not impose "strict scrutiny" standards for the lower courts to assess school board plans for coming into compliance with "the fundamental principle that racial discrimination in public education is unconstitutional." Nor did the Court explain why it is "constitutionally permissible" to delay compliance.[38] Rather, it advised that "[i]n fashioning and effectuating the decrees, the courts will be guided by equitable principles . . . characterized by a practical flexibility in shaping . . . remedies and by a facility for adjusting and reconciling *public* and *private* needs."[39]

III

The Court did not say which principles of equity were to guide the lower courts. It merely referred to two opinions, neither of which had anything to do with constitutional rights or interests. It first cited *Alexander v. Hillman*,[40] a case about the resolution in a court of equity of a dispute concerning the distribution of corporate assets fraudulently withheld by the directors. The Court cited *Alexander*, not for purposes of identifying any "equitable principles," but to make the point that "equity has been characterized by a practical flexibility in shaping its remedies."[41] The Court made no reference to any part of the *Alexander* opinion that explained the equitable factor calling for flexibility in shaping a remedy. In that opinion is found what would seem to be relevant to the *Brown* cases (if, indeed, anything in the *Alexander* opinion is relevant): "Causes of action arising from transgressions of officers and directors of corporations such as those on which the receivers rest their counterclaims are cognizable in equity ... because respondents, ... fraudulently obtained defendant's property and therefore cannot in equity and good conscience retain it."[42]

For *Brown II*, the real but ignored meaning of *Alexander* is that those school systems that had complied with only the "separate" prong of the "separate and equal" reading of the Equal Protection Clause expounded in *Plessy* would be coming to equity with "unclean hands." Thus the school boards in the South Carolina, Virginia, Delaware, and District of Columbia cases might not be entitled to the "practical flexibility" that equity allows. Those school systems, in essence, had been engaged in "fraudulently" obtaining and using funds for white schools that were meant to go to black schools by failing to share available funds equally, even if separately. The Court's use of *Alexander* obscured, rather than revealed, what "equitable principles" might become operative. "Practical flexibility" in the service of equity in fashioning remedies was turned around to mean the invocation of equity jurisdiction in the service of "practical flexibility" in fashioning remedies, however inequitable.

The Court cited only one other opinion on equity, not for guiding principles, but for another merely descriptive proposition to reinforce the "practical flexibility" concept. Equity, the *Brown II* Court said, referring to *Hecht Co. v. Bowles*,[43] is characterized "by a facility for adjusting and reconciling public and private needs."[44] *Hecht*, addressing a statutory rather than a constitutional question, asked whether Congress had intended to afford "a full opportunity for equity courts to treat enforcement proceedings under the [Emergency Price Control Act of 1942] in accordance with their traditional practices, as conditioned by the necessities of the public interest."[45] Who represented the public and who the private interest was in that case, unlike in the *Brown* cases, clear to the Court. Under such circumstances, the *Hecht* Court said:

> The essence of equity jurisdiction has been the power of the Chancellor to do equity to mould each decree to the necessities of the particular case. Flexibility rather than rigidity has distinguished it. The qualities of mercy and practicality have made equity the instrument for nice ad-

justment and reconciliation between the public interest
and private needs as well as between competing private
claims.[46]

The *Hecht* case provided little or no guidance to courts
of equity for understanding how to distinguish between
public and private interests and needs.

The *public* interest in ensuring equal protection of
the law for every schoolchild, white and black alike,
was converted by *Brown II* into an exclusively *private*
black need. The *private* interest of white school board
members seeking to minimize the possible "painful"
consequences for white children and their parents of
having to share on an equitable basis inferior black
schools—inferior because many of the school authorities in these cases had for so long been acting uncon-
stitutionally—was converted into a *public* need. The
Court's confusion of the *public* and the *private* may be
traced to its recognition in *McLaurin* and *Sweatt* of
each claimant's *personal* interest and thus *private* need
to vindicate a violation of his or her constitutional right.
Many *personal* interests are *private* interests; yet *personal* interests of a constitutional dimension are *public*
interests, even if *private*. Without acknowledgment,
the Court blurred this critical distinction. It simply
explained:

> In fashioning and effectuating the decrees, the courts will
> be guided by equitable principles. Traditionally, equity has
> been characterized by a practical flexibility in shaping its
> remedies and by a facility for adjusting and reconciling

public and *private* needs.... At stake is the *personal* interest of the plaintiffs in admission to public schools as soon as practicable on a nondiscriminatory basis. To effectuate this interest may call for elimination of a variety of obstacles in making the transition to school systems operated in accordance with the constitutional principles set forth in our May 17, 1954, decision. Courts of equity may properly take into account the *public* interest in the elimination of such obstacles in a systematic and effective manner. But it should go without saying that the vitality of these constitutional principles cannot be allowed to yield simply because of disagreement with them.

While giving weight to these *public* and *private* considerations, the courts will require that the defendants make a prompt and reasonable start toward full compliance with our May 17, 1954, ruling. Once such a start has been made, the courts may find that additional time is necessary to carry out the ruling in an effective manner. The burden rests upon the defendants to establish that such time is necessary in the *public* interest and is consistent with good faith compliance at the earliest practicable date.[47]

By thus confusing *public* and *private*, the Court failed to clarify what it is that the lower courts, as courts of equity, were to address. It did not force into view the question of whether the black children or the white children were to bear (or to share) the burden of schooling by less qualified staffs in inferior facilities during the period of transition to a nonsegregated school system. The Court did not ask the lower courts to consider whether children who had been deprived and were being deprived of their constitutional right might be assigned to the better "white" schools and their better qualified teachers, or whether they might be deprived of such access so as not to burden white students by assigning some of them to the "black" facilities. Rather, the Court set a focus for the courts of first instance that shielded such problems from their view as matters for resolution in equity. Those courts, in response to requests for delay in compliance,

> may consider problems related to administration, arising from the physical condition of the school plant, the school transportation system, personnel, revision of school districts and attendance areas into compact units to achieve a system of determining admission to the public schools on a nonracial basis, and revision of local laws and regulations which may be necessary in solving the foregoing problems.[48]

The Court accepted, without reasons and without explicit acknowledgment, the notion that the right to equal protection may yield to "administrative" problems that might make compliance particularly painful or troublesome to those who have "benefited" from the denial of equal protection to others. Having left so much unsaid, the Court, almost as an afterthought, observed, "But it should go without saying that the vitality of these constitutional principles cannot be allowed to yield simply because of disagreement with them."[49] Yet it authorized the curtailment of a fundamental constitutional right, a personal-public and not purely personal-private interest, in favor of a primarily group-private and not group-public interest in resolving "administrative problems of considerable complexity." Put somewhat differently, the Court's less than meticulous use of "public," "personal," and "private" invited the authorities to assert the importance of a white public's private interest in not subjecting white children to the inferior "black" schools over the importance of the public-personal constitutional interest in ensuring that at least the black children should not be compelled to remain segregated in the inferior schools. The Court seemed to assume, though it did not say so, that black children alone must bear, not share, the entire burden of any delay when the "public" interest outweighs the "private." Nor did the Court call to the attention of the parties and the lower courts that in the *Sweatt* case, cited in *Brown I*, it had stated:

> It is fundamental that these cases concern rights which are personal and present. This Court has stated unanimously that "The State must provide [legal education] for [petitioner] in conformity with the equal protection clause of the Fourteenth Amendment and provide it as soon as it does for applicants of any other group."[50]

It thus avoided having to explain why the same rights are for schoolchildren any less fundamental, any less personal, or any less present, or why the state is not required to provide public-school education in conformity with the Equal Protection Clause "as soon as it does for [students] of any other group."

The Court might possibly have had or been able to fashion a principled basis for making its public–private distinctions, but it did not offer one. It never justified its call for "practical flexibility." It did not openly explain what it covertly determined about the issues that counsel for the plaintiffs raised in their arguments to the Court.[51] Nor did the Court in *Brown II* explain, particularly for the courts and parties in the District of Columbia, why any desegregation plan that permits curtailing "the civil rights of a single racial group" is *not* necessarily "immediately suspect," requiring under *Korematsu* "the most rigid scrutiny." Any such plan would be justifiable only for "[p]ressing public necessity" but never out of "racial antagonism."[52] The Court, relying on *Korematsu*, did say in *Bolling*: "Classifications based solely upon race must be scrutinized with particular care, since they are contrary to our traditions and hence constitutionally suspect."[53] But the Court in *Brown II*, even though it incorporated *Bolling*, did not squarely address why such constitutional concerns need not guide courts of equity in fashioning remedies.

The reader of the *Brown* opinions does not discover where in the Constitution or in statutory law the authority to sanction proven violations of constitutional rights is to be found. Nor does the reader learn what principles of equity entitle a court to favor a party who comes with "unclean hands" seeking delay for resolving administrative complexities caused primarily by failure to comply in good faith with what, long before *Brown*,

was minimally required of school systems under the
Equal Protection Clause. Of course, had the physical
plant, the teaching staff, the curricula, and the transportation for all the schools, both black and white, been
equal though separate all along, the administrative complexities that the Court found legitimate to consider
would have been substantially reduced. Further, the
Court did not frame its questions in a sufficiently direct
way either to provide principled guidance for balancing
the equities, thus making comprehensible the choice
between conflicting *public* and *private* interests, or to
declare that it could provide no such guidance. As a
result, and "most fundamentally," as Charles Black has
observed of the opinion in *Brown II*, "there was asked
of the laity [We the People] an understanding of which
lawyers are scarcely capable—an understanding that
something could be unlawful [unconstitutional], while
it was nevertheless lawful [constitutional] to continue
it for an indefinite time."[54]

Had the Court in formulating questions for the
hearing in *Brown II* observed "descriptive scrupulousness,"[55] it might have avoided writing an opinion that
could only confuse We the black and white People,
particularly the schoolchitldren whose constitutional
rights it had already declared were being violated and
whose rights, it now declared, might continue to be
violated for some time to come.

The lack of "descriptive scrupulousness" does not
warrant the conclusion that the parties did not "understand" from the Court's opinion that the plaintiffs

were to be denied immediate relief for the already established violations of their constitutional right to equal
protection of the laws. That was made clear in *Brown
I* by the Court's refusal to grant immediate relief until
the following fall, when it would hear additional arguments on remedy. It was also made clear in *Brown
II* by the Court's decision to allow time—"all deliberate
speed"—in which "to effectuate a transition to a racially nondiscriminatory school system."[56]

What these unanimous opinions left unclear—indeed, failed to address—was the constitutional authority for the Court even to contemplate allowing, let
alone to allow, violations of constitutional rights to go
unremedied for an indefinite time. The Court's opinion
in *Brown II* failed to reveal either the constitutional
principles or the principles of equity that were to be
used to identify and then to weigh competing interests.
The Court failed to identify the public interests that
may be weighed against constitutional rights; it also
failed to determine what process is due before the
Court, or indeed a school system, may postpone or deny
relief to persons whose constitutional rights the Court
has held are being violated. In effect, the Court failed
to establish a state interest sufficiently compelling to
justify what the lower courts might do on remand. The
Court seemed to have forgotten that in expounding
the Constitution, it, like the other branches of state
and federal government, is subject to constitutional
restraints.

To resolve the right-remedy issues before it, the

Court would have had to confront and either adopt or explicitly reject constitutional principles, not unlike those that Justice Black articulated in a case involving prior restraint of a newspaper's right to publish under the First Amendment.[57] To paraphrase his words as they might apply to the "prior" and continuing restraint of the schoolchildren's rights under the Fourteenth and Fifth Amendments:

We believe every moment's continuance of the segregation of students by race in the public-school system amounts to a flagrant, indefensible, and continuing violation of the Fourteenth and Fifth Amendments. Unfortunately, the Court did not recognize this before ordering a reargument to determine whether the Negro children concerned should forthwith be admitted to the schools of their choice, or whether the Court may, in the exercise of its equity powers, permit an effective gradual adjustment to be brought about from existing segregated systems to a system not based on color distinctions. In posing these questions, we apparently implied that the Court had, as a court of equity, the constitutional authority to hold that the violation of a personal and present constitutional right to attend a nonsegregated school need sometimes not be enjoined. **Such a holding makes a shambles of the equal-protection rights of Negro children.**[58]

Brown II, without reasons and by implication only, rejected such a position. Thus in one of its most sig-

nificant constitutional decisions, the Court failed to remember that it was expounding the Constitution.

Not far below the surface, and not faced with
candor, was the Court's fear that an order to admit the
children in these cases to the schools of their choice
would be resisted and that the Court's authority would
be undermined.[59] To make this observation is not to
suggest that the Supreme Court ought to be insulated
from real-world pressures. Nor is it to argue that an-
ticipated resistance to the Court's expounding of the
Constitution should be ignored or should never be
taken into account. Rather, it is to argue that the need
to make the opinion in *Brown II* understandable required that to the extent such matters were taken into
account, they should have been forthrightly
acknowledged.

If nationwide or "Southwide" resistance to implementing the holding of the Court in *Brown I* and
Bolling led the Court in *Brown II* to fashion a "remedy"
that tolerated the continuing violation of the constitutional rights of the schoolchildren in these cases, this
logic demanded explanation. The Court might have
found that it could not rely on the relevant state, local,
and federal executive agencies to implement its ruling,
and that it had to alter its constitutionally mandated
course rather than assume the risk of being flouted by
the mob.[60] The Court might then have been forced to
consider whether the relief granted would have been
different if the power of coercion and violence was not
solely in the white community, but also in the black
community.

Of course, courts would and should find it unprincipled to act out of such concerns and thus difficult, if not impossible, to acknowledge openly in their opinions that they had done so. But to give covertly the "hecklers' veto" to the resisters is no less unprincipled and no less a challenge to the Court's authority and integrity. Yet the Court, while saying that "it should go without saying that the vitality of these constitutional principles cannot be allowed to yield simply because of disagreement with them," took these matters into account under the cloak of equity.[61] It turned the introduction of equity in constitutional adjudication out of "our desire for justice"[62] into a means of perpetuating injustice and weakening the fundamental constitutional notion that our government is "emphatically ... a government of laws."[63]

In the closing paragraphs of *Brown II*, the Court appears to have shifted its focus from a nationwide perspective to local perspectives—to "the parties to these cases" and controversies.[64] But the Court failed to consider the varied local conditions in which the five *Brown* cases arose. It simply remanded each case to the courts below "to take such proceedings and enter such orders and decrees consistent with this opinion as are necessary and proper to admit to public schools on a racially nondiscriminatory basis *with all deliberate speed* the parties to these cases."[65] Though the Court treated separately, it did not treat differently the 1952 Delaware judgment ordering the "immediate admission [of the plaintiffs] to schools previously attended only by white children."[66] While affirming the decision, the

Court in *Brown II* did not reinstate the order. Rather, it remanded the case "to the Supreme Court of Delaware for such further proceedings as that Court may deem necessary in light of this opinion."[67] "Immediate admission" was thus replaced with an indeterminate "with all deliberate speed."

The Court spoke in *Brown*, as it did later in *Cooper*, with unanimity, possibly to avoid the confusion associated with multiple opinions. Yet the Court did not speak in a single voice. Reading the three *Brown* opinions as one, as the Court advised, We the People and the courts below are left confused by an initial unequivocal holding of constitutional violations followed by an equivocal "with all deliberate speed" guide that purportedly granted, but in fact denied, the plaintiffs' constitutional rights.[68]*

*These observations cannot, and certainly are not meant to, detract from the powerful symbolic force of the Court's opinion in *Brown I*. But they do prompt asking whether the actual realization of the values symbolized by *Brown I* would have been better served had the Court not separated the constitutional principle it expounded from the remedy it was to fashion for its violation. In a communication to the American Academy of Arts and Sciences in January 1988, Justice Stevens said that he shared the view of District Judge Charles Wyzanski, who had written about the part Justice Frankfurter played in *Brown*: "If F.F. had not persuaded Warren, C.J. and the others to put off the decree in the case and instead to have incorporated the mischievous phrase from ancient English equity practice ... 'WITH ALL DELIBERATE SPEED' ... THERE WOULD HAVE RAPIDLY BEEN 100% COMPLIANCE IN THE SOUTH AS WELL AS ELSEWHERE." Stevens, The Concept of Liberty, 41 *Bull.: Am. Acad. Arts & Sci.* 11, 30 (1988).

CHAPTER 5

FAILING TO TAKE THEIR OWN AND EACH OTHER'S OPINIONS SERIOUSLY

Regents of the University of California v. Bakke

In 1970, the medical school at the University of California at Davis inaugurated a special admissions program for "disadvantaged or minority" students. Under the program, 16 of the 100 places in each entering class were set aside for "Blacks," "Chicanos," "Asians," and "American Indians."[1] As a result, white students, because of their race, were not entitled, as were minority students, to compete for all 100 places. Alan Bakke, a white, twice sought admission. Though he ranked higher, by the school's standards, than many of those admitted via the separate track for the "disadvantaged," he was rejected on each occasion.

Bakke sued the Regents of the University of California, claiming a violation of his rights under the Equal Protection Clause of the Fourteenth Amendment to the Constitution and under Section 601 of Title VI of the Civil Rights Act of 1964. Title VI, which applied to the medical school as a recipient of federal funds, provides: "No person...shall, on the ground of race, color, or national origin, be excluded from participation in, be denied the benefits of, or be subjected to discrimination under any program or activity receiving Federal financial assistance."[2] The Fourteenth Amendment states: "No State shall...deny to any person within its jurisdiction the equal protection of the laws."

The Supreme Court of California held that the special admissions program violated both Title VI and the Equal Protection Clause. It enjoined the medical school "from taking race into account in any way in making admissions decisions"[3] and directed the lower court to order Bakke's admission.

On appeal to the United States Supreme Court, both the medical school and Bakke, in their competing claims, called for statutory as well as constitutional interpretations. The focus of this chapter is primarily, though not exclusively, on the Court's work in exposition of the Constitution's Equal Protection Clause. It took 6 separate opinions, totaling 156 pages with 167 footnotes, to answer (or to leave unanswered) the constitutional questions posed.

I

Justice Stevens, in a thirteen-page opinion for himself, Chief Justice Burger, Justice Stewart, and Justice Rehnquist, determined that the two-track "special admissions program" violated Title VI and that constitutional issues need not be addressed in order to decide Bakke's claim. Thus the Stevens four did not consider whether the specific "special admissions program" was unconstitutional or, if it was, whether race may ever be used as a factor in admissions under the Equal Protection Clause.

Justice Brennan, in a fifty-five-page opinion for himself and for Justices White, Marshall, and Blackmun (each of whom also wrote a separate opinion), determined that the "special admissions program" did not violate the Fourteenth Amendment, that "Title VI goes no further in prohibiting the use of race than the Equal Protection Clause,"[4] and that therefore the use of race in affirmative admission programs is permissible.

Justice Powell, in a fifty-four-page opinion, provided the basis for two separate Court judgments—one a majority with the Stevens four and the other a majority with the Brennan four. Like Justice Brennan, Justice Powell concluded that "Title VI must be held to proscribe only those racial classifications that would violate the Equal Protection Clause."[5] Like Justice Brennan, though not to the same extent, he concluded that "race may be taken into account as a factor in an admissions program."[6] But unlike Justice Brennan, he concluded that the Davis "special admissions program" did violate the Equal Protection Clause and consequently violated Title VI as well.[7]*

At the start of his opinion, Justice Powell announced the Court's two 5 to 4 judgments. The first judgment held that the "special admissions program" was "unlawful."[8] The second judgment held that the California Supreme Court's "judgment enjoining [the medical school] from according any consideration to race in its admissions process must be reversed."[9] Justice Powell introduced each judgment without explanation. He merely referred to "the reasons stated" in his opinion and to "the reasons expressed" in the separate opinions of the other justices.[10]

By failing to explain the reasons on which each Court judgment rested, Justice Powell left a vacuum that Justice Brennan attempted to fill. Recognizing the confusion that must attend judgments resting on "many opinions, no single one speaking for the Court,"[11] Justice Brennan opened his opinion with a plea that the "central meaning" of the opinions not be masked by their multiplicity. He declared, presumably with regard to the second judgment:

---

*Justice Powell wrote, "The guarantee of equal protection cannot mean one thing when applied to one individual and something else when applied to a person of another color. If both are not accorded the same protection, then it is not equal." *Regents of the University of California v. Bakke*, 438 U.S. 265, 289–290 (1978).

> [T]he central meaning of today's opinions [is that] Gov-
> ernment may take race into account when it acts not to
> demean or insult any racial group, but to remedy disad-
> vantages cast on minorities by past racial prejudice, at
> least when appropriate findings have been made by ju-
> dicial, legislative, or administrative bodies with compe-
> tence to act in this area.[12]

Rather than remain silent, Justice Powell should
have indicated whether or not he agreed with the "central meaning" statement. Had he agreed, Justice Powell
might have suggested to Justice Brennan, prior to hand-
ing down the Court's decision, something like the
following:

Your "central meaning" paragraph properly belongs in
my opinion. You have captured the constitutional principle on which the second judgment rests. Though we
read the Equal Protection Clause differently, you describe an area of agreement between us about its meaning. Indeed, I will go further. I will explain that though
the Stevens four do not decide the constitutional questions before us, they do acknowledge that our "central
meaning" statement accurately reflects the common
constitutional ground on which the Court's second judgment rests.

But Justice Powell did not include this or any other
"central meaning" statement in his announcement of

the judgments.* And Justice Stevens forthrightly, albeit in a textual footnote, called into question the undertaking of the Brennan four "to announce the legal and constitutional effect of the Court's judgment."[13] He wrote, "It is hardly necessary to state that only a majority can speak for the Court or determine what is the 'central meaning' of any judgment of the Court."[14†]

In announcing the Court's first judgment, Justice Powell abided by his judicial obligation to represent accurately what the Court decided. Recognizing that he was the only member of the majority—indeed, the only member of the Court—to hold that the program violated the Equal Protection Clause, he was careful to say that a majority concluded that the "special admissions program" was "unlawful" rather than "unconstitutional." However, instead of the uninformative "for reasons expressed," Justice Powell should have explained that "unlawful" was used deliberately because the Court's judgment rested on the votes of the Stevens four, who relied solely on their reading of Title VI and

---

*This omission seems ironic in light of Justice Powell's emphasis in his opinion on the importance of "coherent interpretation" and his statement that in "expounding the Constitution, the Court's role is to discern 'principles sufficiently absolute to give them roots throughout the community and continuity over significant periods of time, and to lift them above the level of the pragmatic political judgments of a particular time and place.' " *Regents of the University of California v. Bakke*, 438 U.S. 265, 299 (1978) (quoting A. Cox, *The Role of the Supreme Court in American Government* (1976), 114).

†On the undesirability of relegating to footnotes material that is directly related to the meaning of the holding, see Chapter 6, especially the fifth canon of comprehensibility offered there.

who stated explicitly that their statutory interpretation obviated the need to consider the constitutional questions raised.

Had Justice Powell been less meticulous and less serious in reading the opinions of his colleagues and more intent on having it appear that his own reading of the Equal Protection Clause had the support of the Court, he could have written in announcing the first judgment:

The central meaning of today's opinions is that the special admissions program is unconstitutional. Since I and the Brennan four agree that Title VI proscribes only those racial classifications that would violate the Equal Protection Clause,[15] and since I and the Stevens four agree that the special admissions program violates Title VI,[16] it follows that Bakke's exclusion—because of his race—from competing for all seats in the entering class at Davis is a violation of his rights under the Fourteenth Amendment, not just his rights under Title VI.

Only perverse logic would permit such a reading. Each justice and any serious reader of the 151 opinion pages would agree that such a statement would disinform. It would be false, even though grounded in verifiable positions that may be attributed to the opinions. It fails to take those opinions seriously and thus avoids the whole truth—which is that eight of the nine justices rejected this view. The Stevens four explicitly declined

to determine the constitutionality of the program. The
Brennan four concluded that the "special admissions
program" did not violate the Equal Protection Clause.
Only one justice, Justice Powell—not the Court—held
that the program violated Bakke's "personal rights" under the Fourteenth Amendment.[17]

Justice Brennan's "central meaning" statement
does not satisfy the accuracy requirements applied to,
and clearly unmet by, the hypothetical Powell statement concerning the Court's first judgment. Justice
Brennan did not speak for the Court. To speak for the
Court, which no single opinion in *Bakke* did, the "central meaning" statement by the Brennan four required
that Justice Powell explicitly accept it as an accurate
or fair reading of his opinion. He did not.

As already noted, the statement attributed to the
Court's opinions, presumably including the Stevens
opinion, was the proposition that "[g]overnment may
take race into account when it acts not to demean or
insult any racial group, but to remedy disadvantages
cast on minorities by past racial prejudice, at least when
appropriate findings have been made by judicial, legislative, or administrative bodies with competence to
act in this area."[18] But Justice Powell did not accept
this proposition. While agreeing that race may be taken
into account in admissions programs, he observed, also
in a textual footnote:

In the view of MR. JUSTICE BRENNAN, MR. JUSTICE WHITE,
MR. JUSTICE MARSHALL, and MR. JUSTICE BLACKMUN, the pli-

able notion of "stigma" is the crucial element in analyzing racial classifications.... The Equal Protection Clause is not framed in terms of "stigma." Certainly the word has no clearly defined constitutional meaning. It reflects a subjective judgment that is standardless.... Moreover, [the Brennan four] offer no principle for deciding whether preferential classifications reflect a benign remedial purpose or a malevolent stigmatic classification, since they are willing...to accept mere...declarations by an isolated state entity—a medical school faculty—unadorned by particularized findings of past discrimination, to establish such a remedial purpose.[19]*

The words that appear to speak for a Court majority on whether race may sometimes be taken into account are found in Justice Powell's opinion. The Brennan four explicitly joined those words, which say: "[T]he State has a substantial interest that legitimately may be served by a properly devised admissions program involving the competitive consideration of race and ethnic origin."[20] For Justice Powell, the interest that is "substantial enough to support the use of a suspect classification"[21] in an admissions program "is the attainment of a diverse student body."[22] He emphasized that such diversity is not "simple ethnic diversity, in

---

*Except for the "central meaning" statement, Justice Brennan did not use the words "demean" and "insult," and neither did Justice Powell. Rather, Justice Brennan substituted the language of "stigma" "that causes fatality" under the Fourteenth Amendment, of being "stamped as inferior," or of having "inflict[ed] a pervasive injury." *Regents of the University of California v. Bakke*, 438 U.S. 360–362, 373–375 (1978) (Brennan, White, Marshall, and Blackmun, JJ., concurring in the judgment in part and dissenting in part).

which a specified percentage of the student body is in effect guaranteed to be members of selected ethnic groups,"[23] but that it "encompasses a far broader array of qualifications and characteristics of which racial or ethnic origin is but a single though important element."[24]

Justice Powell's views on "stigma" and on when government may take race into account, as well as the entire tone of his opinion, explain why he could not concur with the "central meaning" statement. In a footnote, he expressed agreement with the Brennan four "that the portion of the [California court's] judgment that would proscribe all consideration of race must be reversed."[25] He went on to emphasize:

> ...I disagree with much that is said in their opinion.
>
> They would require as a justification for a program such as [the medical school's] only two findings: (i) that there has been some form of discrimination against the preferred minority group by "society at large" (it has been conceded that [the medical school] had no history of discrimination), and (ii) that "there is reason to believe" that the disparate impact sought to be rectified by the program is the "product" of such discrimination.
>
> .   .   .
>
> The breadth of this hypothesis is unprecedented in our constitutional system. The first step is easily taken. No one denies the regrettable fact that there has been societal discrimination in this country against various racial and ethnic groups. The second step, however, involves a speculative leap: but for this discrimination by society

at large, Bakke "would have failed to qualify for admission" because Negro applicants—nothing is said about Asians—would have made better scores. Not one word in the record supports this conclusion, and the authors of the opinion offer no standard for courts to use in applying such a presumption of causation to other racial or ethnic classifications. This failure is a grave one.

Only by concluding that Justice Powell did not mean what he said, only by *not* taking his opinion seriously, could the Brennan four represent that he shared with them their statement of the central meaning of *Bakke*.[26] And by failing to disavow explicitly that statement, Justice Powell, unlike Justice Stevens, risked leaving the impression that it spoke with precedential authority.

Ideally, all members of the Court, including those who dissent or who concur for reasons not shared by the majority, should be able to attest to the accuracy of such "central meaning" statements. They ought to feel obligated to report with scrupulous care what it is that they attribute to the opinion of another justice and, most particularly, to the opinion of the Court expounding the Constitution. Such readings are essential to maintaining the integrity of the Court and the reliability of its communications.*

Everything the Court does rests on language. Words matter. They must be used with care. We the People

---

*The obligation to be accurate would apply as well to the reading of prior decisions of the Court, whether a justice draws on them for support or singles them out for overruling.

are expected to rely on the justices' opinions as written. Generally, we are not and ought not to be able to go behind the scenes to read draft opinions and to examine communications among the justices during their deliberations in a specific case. An opinion should stand on its own.

II

Communications between the justices in the preparation of an opinion—however interesting to the scholar—should not be used to interpret an opinion. As authority, such exchanges are even more suspect than is "legislative history" in statutory interpretation.[27] In *Behind Bakke*, Bernard Schwartz permits us, however, to examine some of the exchanges between Justices Powell and Brennan concerning the "central meaning" statement, which, up to this point, I have analyzed solely on the basis of the official opinions in the case. These exchanges support the view that the justices feel themselves obligated to be accurate while, at the same time, they may blind themselves to their own failings or remain publicly silent about the misreading of their views by another justice.

In May 1978, Justice Brennan wrote to Justice Powell:

I have read your opinion very carefully and have regretfully come to the conclusion that I should write out my own views.... [They] differ so substantially from your own that no common ground seems possible.[28]

In June, Justice Brennan circulated a draft of his opinion that suggests that he may have found some "common ground." In the opening paragraph, he wrote:

> [T]he central meaning of this Court's judgment [is that] Government may take race into account when it acts not to demean or insult any racial group, but to remedy disadvantages cast on minorities by past racial prejudice.[29]

Later he telephoned Justice Powell to ask, Professor Schwartz reports, "whether this sentence was accurate as to Powell's opinion as well as Brennan's."[30] In a letter dated June 23, Justice Powell replied:

> If your statement is read literally, I doubt that it does reflect accurately the judgment of the Court. In terms of "judgment," my opinion is limited to holding that a state university validly may consider race to achieve diversity. ... [M]y opinion recognizes broadly (perhaps one could call it dicta) that consideration of race is appropriate to eliminate the effects of past discrimination *when appropriate findings have been made* by judicial, legislative, or administrative bodies *authorized* to act.[31]

Justice Brennan, apparently responding to some of Justice Powell's observations, though not necessarily to his real concerns, changed the wording of his draft statement in two ways. First, he modified the initial few words to read "the central meaning of today's opinions" rather than "the central meaning of this Court's judgment." This substitution of "opinions" for "judgment"

removes whatever technical objection there may have
been to speaking about the central meaning of the
Court's judgment. But it is unresponsive to the substantive issues raised by Justice Powell. Second, Justice
Brennan added at the end of his initial statement: "[A]t
least when appropriate findings have been made by
judicial, legislative, or administrative bodies *with competence* to act."[32] By using "at least" in his modification
rather than "only" or another qualification to "when
appropriate findings have been made," he temporized
or took away the limited reading that Justice Powell
gave to the Equal Protection Clause and the restraint
that Justice Powell believed it places on state government. By substituting "with competence" for "authorized," Justice Brennan enlarged rather than restricted,
as Justice Powell would have it, the source from which
the crucial findings of past racial prejudice might come.

Justice Powell's letter left no doubt that the original "central meaning" statement permitted more than
his opinion would allow and suggested more than he
intended to say. Yet none of Justice Brennan's modi-
fications served his stated goal of accuracy. Justice
Powell wrote:

> [T]he *judgment* itself does not go beyond permissible use
> of race in the context of achieving a diverse student body
> at a state university. This holding could be stated more
> broadly in one single sentence as follows: "Government
> validly may take race into account in furthering the com-
> pelling state interest of achieving a diverse student
> body."[33]

Meticulous scrupulousness, respect for the notion that opinions by members of the Court are to be taken seriously, and recognition of the significance of precedent and of the importance of *stare decisis* should have led Justice Brennan to say no more in his "central meaning" statement than can be drawn from that single sentence. It was the only "common ground," if indeed there was any, on which the second judgment rests.

Justice Brennan, as we know, did say more, possibly because the closing words of Justice Powell's letter allowed him to abandon his stated goal of accuracy or to blind himself to inaccuracy. With characteristic civility, and apparently without recognizing that personal feelings of collegiality may sometimes obscure professional responsibilities, Justice Powell wrote:

> Despite the foregoing, I have not objected to your characterization of what the Court holds as I have thought you could put whatever "gloss" on the several opinions you think proper. I believe that one who reads my opinion carefully will conclude that your gloss goes somewhat beyond what I have written and what I think....In sum, while I might prefer that you describe the judgment differently, I have not thought of making any response on this point beyond what I have already circulated.[34]

Justice Powell's permissive comments seem to have subverted the function of Justice Brennan's inquiry. Justice Powell informed him that his " 'gloss' goes somewhat beyond what I have written and what I think." That should have been enough to cause Justice

Brennan to abandon his "central meaning" statement
or to modify it more carefully, more responsibly, than
he did. But Justice Powell added, as if this were nothing
more than a personal, as opposed to a professional,
exchange, "you could put whatever 'gloss'...you think
proper" on my opinion. He indicated that he would say
nothing more about this matter. Apparently, Justice
Powell felt assured that the integrity of the judgment
and of the Court was not being jeopardized because
"one who *reads my opinion carefully* will conclude
that your gloss goes somewhat beyond what I have
written and what I think."[35] It is as if Justice Powell
were saying to Justice Brennan and those who joined
his opinion:

You need not take my opinion too seriously. You may
give it less than a careful reading, for I am confident
that those who read it carefully will discover that you
have misunderstood what I say about how and why race
may be taken into account in fashioning admissions programs without violating the Equal Protection Clause.

Rather than rely on state and federal court judges,
lawyers, and We the People to read his opinion more
"carefully" than did Justice Brennan, Justice Powell
should have taken his own opinion more seriously. In
order to remove the troublesome gloss of the "central
meaning" statement, Justice Powell should have insisted that words not be put in his opinion, even indi-

rectly, that were not there, that change its meaning. Furthermore, he should have included in his opinion his own unpublished "simple" statement of his holding:

> Government validly may take race into account in furthering the compelling state interest of achieving a diverse student body.[36]

Whether that is the way the Court should have read the Equal Protection Clause is not the point. The point is that the Court, as a majority, could not be said to have held anything more than that in reaching the second judgment. Put another way, the "central meaning" statement is a comprehensible articulation of a constitutional principle that the Court might have expounded. Yet, when read in context, it misinforms. Justices Powell and Brennan, engaged in a discussion to ensure accuracy, somehow lost sight of their obligation to each other, to the entire Court, and to We the People.

III

Apparently, the justices in *Bakke* recognized that their many opinions, totaling 151 pages, failed as a communication to and for We the People. Justice Powell drafted and circulated a "Proposed Statement from Bench," which he gave orally in announcing the *Bakke* decision. In an accompanying memo, he wrote, "My primary purpose was to assist the representatives of the media present in understanding 'what in the world' the Court has done!"[37] It was as if he were acknowledging that the Court's public is to be informed not primarily by the opinions of the Court, but by the media, and that professional law correspondents cannot, by reading the opinion alone, be expected to understand what the Court has decided and why.

Justice Powell's oral statement is the kind of communication that would satisfy the demand placed on the justices not to forget that it is a constitution they are expounding. Yet it has no authoritative value. It was not even published.[38] One can only wonder why it did not find a place in (or take the place of) his official opinion announcing the Court's two judgments. From the bench, he said:

> ...As there are six separate opinions, and the judgment itself is a bifurcated one, I will try at the outset to explain the judgment.
>
> The opinion and judgment of the Supreme Court of California presented us with two central questions: the first—and the one widely perceived as the only ultimate question—is whether the medical school's special admissions program discriminated unlawfully against Bakke, either under the Constitution or Title VI of the Civil Rights Act of 1964. I will refer to this as the Bakke admission question.
>
> The second, and broader question, is whether it is ever permissible to consider race as a factor relevant to the admission of applicants to a university. I will refer to this question, generally, as whether race may be considered.

... [I]f the answer to the second question is negative—that is, that race may never validly be considered, this answer disposes of both issues. Bakke would be admitted, and the University could not in the future give any consideration to race in its admission program.

If, however, the second question is answered affirmatively—that is, that race may be considered—then it becomes necessary also to address the first question separately: that is whether the special admissions program at Davis is compatible with Title VI and the Constitution.

I have mentioned both Title VI—often referred to as the "statutory issue"—and the Constitution, under which is presented the equal protection issue arising under the Fourteenth Amendment. Again, the case is complicated because if it were disposed of under Title VI, there would be no occasion to reach the constitutional issues.

Now, as to how the questions are decided:

Mr. Justice Stevens, joined by the Chief Justice, and Justices Stewart and Rehnquist, concludes that Title VI does control. As he will state more fully, Mr. Justice Stevens concludes that Bakke was excluded from Davis in violation of Title VI. His plurality opinion therefore concurs in the Court's judgment insofar as it affirms the judgment of the California Court ordering that Bakke be admitted.

Justices Brennan, White, Marshall, Blackmun and I have a different view as to Title VI. We believe, despite its more detailed provisions, that it goes no further in prohibiting the use of race than the Equal Protection Clause. The five of us therefore reach both of the consitutional questions.

On a constitutional analysis, founded on the equal protection clause, Justices Brennan, White, Marshall and Blackmun in their joint opinion hold not only that race properly may be considered, but that the special admissions program of the Davis Medical School is valid in every respect.

.   .   .

As I agree that Title VI does not dispose of this case, I also addressed the constitutional questions.

On the first question—whether the special admissions program is invalid—I agree with the result reached by Mr. Justice Stevens' opinion. But I do so on constitutional grounds rather than under Title VI.

Thus there are five votes to affirm the judgment invalidating the special program. Under this judgment, Bakke will be admitted to the medical school.

As to the second constitutional issue—whether race may be considered as a factor in an admissions program—I agree with the result reached by the joint opinion of Mr. Justice Brennan and my Brothers who joined him. Thus, there are five Justices who join in a judgment of reversal on this issue.

But the process of constitutional analysis by which I reach this result differs significantly from that of the four Justices who have filed a joint opinion.

As my reasoning is set forth fully in my written opinion, and as other Justices will speak, I will merely make a brief conclusory statement:

The Davis special admissions program, with 16 of 100 seats reserved exclusively for three categories of minorities, is a classification based on race. Our cases establish, beyond question, that a racial classification is inherently suspect, and must be subjected to the most exacting judicial scrutiny.

Although adopted primarily to protect persons of the Negro race, the guarantee of the Equal Protection Clause—by its terms—protects all "persons." It provides explicitly that no person shall be denied equal protection of the laws.

Despite this absolute language, our cases have held that some distinctions are justified if necessary to further a compelling state interest.

Davis relies on several interests said to be compelling. One is the desire to redress a racial imbalance said to result from general societal discrimination against the minority groups selected for preferential treatment. But there is a complete absence, on this record, of any findings that this imbalance is traceable to discriminatory practices. Discrimination by society at large, with no determined effects, is not sufficient to justify petitioner's racial classification.

In my view, the only interest that fairly may be viewed as compelling on this record is that of a university in a diverse student body.

This interest—encompassed within the concept of academic freedom—is a special concern of the First Amendment. But there has been no showing in this case that the Davis special program is necessary to achieve educational diversity.

The Davis program totally excludes all applicants who are not Negro, Asian or Chicano from 16 of the 100 seats in an entering class. No matter how strong their qualifications, qualitative and quantitative, including their own potential for contributing to educational diversity, they are not afforded the opportunity to compete with applicants from the preferred groups for these 16 seats.

At the same time, the preferred applicants have the opportunity to compete for every seat in the class.

A university's interest in a diverse student body is not limited to ethnic diversity. Rather, its compelling interest in this respect encompasses a far broader array of qualifications and characteristics, of which race is only one.

. . .

[I]n a flexible program designed to achieve diversity, [race] is only one factor—weighed competitively—against a number of other factors deemed relevant....

[E]xperience demonstrates that the Davis-type program—one that arbitrarily forecloses all competition solely on the basis of race or ethnic origin—is not necessary to attain reasonable educational diversity.

[I]t therefore violates the Equal Protection Clause in a most fundamental sense.[39]

This unofficial, unpublished, and succinct statement— far shorter than Justice Powell's fifty-one-page opinion—meets the standard for accuracy in reporting and explaining the basis for the two judgments reached by a divided Court. Indeed, it does more than Justice Powell's opinion to make accessible and comprehensible the constitutional and statutory meaning of the decision. As a communication, it is a model opinion.*

---

*Justice Brennan's oral statement repeated the "central meaning" state-

Only five days before the Court announced its decision, Chief Justice Burger had corrected what he perceived to be an erroneous implication that had slipped into the draft syllabus of the case. The Chief Justice, as Professor Schwartz reports, circulated a memorandum to the conference suggesting changes in the proposed syllabus of the case that the Reporter of Decisions had prepared:

> The most important change suggested was in the draft's statement of the reversal, which read that the judgment below "is reversed insofar as it prohibits petitioner from taking race into account in any way in its future admissions decisions." Burger wrote that this was inaccurate and noted, "I understand from [Justice] Lewis [Powell] that he agrees that the three words 'in any way' overstate the holding. He also indicates he would suggest that these three words be stricken and 'as a factor' be substituted."
>
> "Ordinarily," the Burger memo conceded, "we need not worry unduly about headnotes but with the high tension that has been generated, the headnote in this case is crucial and will guide most of what is written and said on the evening and day following announcement."

The Chief Justice ended his memo by noting, "All these final days are under pressure and it is understandable that problems such as this arise." However, he wrote, it was "imperative" that the headnote be accurate. "At

---

ment, just as it appeared in his published opinion. W. Brennan, Draft of oral statement (Manuscript Division, Library of Congress). Bernard Schwartz provided the author with a copy of the full statement, which he summarizes in *Behind Bakke: Affirmative Action and the Supreme Court* (1988), 146.

best," Burger wryly remarked, "people will be over-whelmed in dealing with this case."[40]

They were.[41]

Surely it should be no less imperative for each justice, not only the Chief Justice, to ensure that any attributions of "central meaning" reflect accurately the basis for the Court's judgment. It was when *Bakke* came down, and still is, a practice of the Court to note that the syllabus that accompanies each opinion "con-stitutes no part of the opinion of the Court but has been prepared by the Reporter of Decisions for the conve-nience of the Court. See *United States v. Detroit Lum-ber Co.*"[42] The government's lawyer in *Detroit Lumber*, relying on the syllabus's headnote, argued that the Court had settled the question before it in a prior de-cision. The Court replied that "the headnote is not the work of the court, nor does it state its decision."[43] Un-fortunately, the same may be said of the "central mean-ing" statement in *Bakke*. It is not the work of the Court. Yet, with the exception of the footnote in the Stevens four concurrence, it stood unchallenged.

PART III

CANONS OF COMPREHENSIBILITY

The studies of opinions in National League of Cities, Garcia, Cooper, Brown, Bolling, *and* Bakke *have been primarily concerned with the individual and collaborative responsibility of the justices for maintaining the Constitution as something that We the People—not just We the specialists, scholars, and practitioners in law and politics—can understand. Each study has addressed the question: Does the opinion or, if more than one, do the opinions in a case, viewed as a single communication by the Court, enable We the People to understand the nature of and reasons for accord and discord among the justices about their rendering of the Constitution?*

These studies lead me to suggest, first, that the justices consider fashioning for themselves canons of comprehensibility to guide their opinion-writing and, second, that on completing but prior to releasing the opinion(s) in a constitutional law case, the justices provide themselves with an occasion to review together, in terms of their canons, what they have written.

CHAPTER 6

TOWARD THE INTELLIGIBLE CONSTITUTION

Opinion-writing is an art. It is highly personal and individualistic as well as collaborative. The authority, if not the authoritativeness, of each opinion rests on the membership of the writing justice in a specially constituted ensemble of nine—the Supreme Court of the United States. Dependent on one another for the Court's performance, each member of this nonet has, like those of a chamber music group, "an independent part equal in importance with the rest."[1] At the same time, the jurist, like the musician, is involved in an endeavor "beyond himself."[2] A justice is not totally free to perform as he or she chooses. To have authority, a justice's rendition of the text must have the support of at least four colleagues. Supreme Court Justice Harlan Fisk Stone, a former law professor and dean, observed that "the university professor is the only free man who can develop legal doctrine in his own way and travel the road he chooses in accounting for his conclusion."[3] It is, however, also a "fact...that the Court functions," as Justice Robert H. Jackson observed, "less as one deliberative body than as nine, each Justice working largely in isolation, except as he chooses to seek consultation with others. These working methods tend to cultivate a highly individualistic rather than group viewpoint."[4] The subtlety and complexity of this joint and independent endeavor are captured in Justice Brennan's interpretation of the traditional preconference shaking of hands by the justices on entering the conference room. "It is a symbol that harmony of aims if not of views is the Court's guiding principle."[5]

The proposal that I make in this chapter—for the Court to formulate canons of comprehensibility to guide its opinion-writing and to develop a practice for reviewing, in terms of its canons, completed opinion(s) before releasing them—is not intended to deprive the justices of their individualistic ways. Rather, it is meant to cultivate greater recognition on their part that each opinion in a constitutional law decision is also to be viewed as part of a whole, as one communication. The goal is not simply that each opinion be coherent by itself, but that, taken together, the opinions in a single case constitute a comprehensible message about the Constitution.

Thus the purpose of a pre-release review of what the justices have written in a case is not to achieve either unanimity or harmony. Rather, it is to ensure that the opinions are clear about the nature and extent of concord and discord among the justices concerning the constitutional issues that they address. And it is to ensure that the Court's public rendering of the Constitution is in a form that can be understood.* To that end, the justices must tap a perception of themselves and of the Court that finds expression in an African proverb, "I am because we are. Because we are, I am."[6] Acting out of a sense of pride in the Court's work, the justices would serve, not sacrifice, the personal recognition that they deserve for the opinions they write. In the context of these notions, I proffer, for purposes of illustration, some canons of comprehensibility and a process for making them operative.

I

In expounding the Constitution, the Court has a task reminiscent of that which the Constitutional Convention's Committees of Detail and Style so successfully performed. Drawing on the drafting goals that the justices have already promulgated, on their own often

---

*Justice Story believed that it was his "duty," except in nonconstitutional law cases, "to give a public expression of [his] opinions, when they differed from that of the Court," writing that "upon constitutional questions, the public have a right to know the opinion of every judge who dissents from the opinion of the Court, and the reasons of his dissent." *Birscoe v. Bank of the Commonwealth of Kentucky*, 36 U.S. (11 Peters) 257, 329, 329, 350 (1837).

implicit notions about good opinion-writing, on studies of their opinions, and on an examination of legal literature, I suggest that the justices "self"-consciously promulgate guidelines for maintaining the intelligibility of the Constitution. These guidelines might take the form of something like the following five overlapping and intertwined canons of comprehensibility.[7]*

1. Use simple and precise language "level to the understanding of all."[8]

"Write it so your Mamma can understand it," Justice Hugo L. Black said to his law clerk on one of those rare occasions when he allowed him to prepare the first draft of an opinion.[9] The goal of this canon is to ensure that opinions make the constitutional bases for decision understandable to the public. It is to ensure the continuing accessibility of the Constitution to the People. It is to serve our commitment to being an intelligent democracy. "[T]he Justices," wrote Eugene V. Rostow, "are inevitably teachers in a vital national seminar."[10] The original and ultimate authority of the Supreme Court in expounding the Constitution lies, after all, with a People thus educated.

Emphasis in this canon on the continuing informed

---

*This is not to suggest that the canons for nonconstitutional law cases would be different or that a final-phase conference in such cases would be inappropriate. It is rather to acknowledge that my proposal rests only on studies of constitutional law opinions and on my reading of the *McCulloch* Court's admonition that the justices not forget it is a constitution they are expounding.

consent of We the People based on comprehensible communications from the Court must not mask the fact that "[i]lliteracy was endemic in the United States at the time the Constitution was ratified and remains so today."[11] Indeed, illiteracy today places an even greater burden on the Court to use simple language than when Marshall was Chief Justice and We the People was more narrowly conceived. As Leon Botstein has observed:

> the egalitarian extension of democratic power and the institution of universal schooling for children and adolescents in the two centuries since 1787 have not been accompanied by an achievement of literacy among the population adequate to the ideal political premises of democracy—the exercise of government by free people through the use of reason and communication and not through the use of violence.[12]

Professor Botstein continues:

> Would an improvement of the bottom level and the elevation of elite standards in a common language actually increase the probabilities that justice, equity, and freedom will flourish? Since what is needed is . . . the development of thought through language throughout the population, this doubt can only be answered with a counterfactual answer. Are we better off not trying? . . . At a minimum, it is reasonably certain that democratic theory depends, for the moment, on the possibility of communication through written as well as spoken literacy.[13]

This canon is meant to keep that possibility alive and thriving by having the justices impose on themselves the obligation to write comprehensible opinions "level to the *understanding* of all."

That many of the People are illiterate makes it no less compelling that the Court's communications about the Constitution be in plain language understandable to the literate. In spoken language, the literate—not only lawyers but also teachers, newspaper reporters, television and radio commentators—must be enabled to inform those who are less literate in order to enable them to speak for themselves. To say this is not to suggest that the Court reinstate the practice of having the justices read aloud their opinions when a decision is announced. Rather, it is to suggest that in this age and day when so much is communicated to so many by word of mouth on radio and television, written opinions be accessible when read aloud.

2. *Write with candor and clarity.*

Justice William O. Douglas captured the principle animating this canon when he wrote, "A judiciary that discloses what it is doing and why it does it will breed understanding. Any confidence based on understanding is more enduring than confidence based on awe."[14] Likewise, Joseph Vining, marking the distinction between authoritarian and authoritative decisions, rhetorically and rightly asked:

Why does the judge write an opinion if not to justify his

decision and his statements? And why would anyone read the opinion if it made no difference whether one was persuaded by it or not? The authority of a legal text is in this sense not automatic. Its authority must be earned too.[15]

Justice Powell, seeking to earn that authority and sensitive to his collegial responsibilities, "insisted," according to one of his law clerks, "that his opinions openly confront opposing arguments, not as a sign of weakness, but as an obligation of candor."[16]

The call for candor—for the "real" and significant reasons underlying the decision—is a response to the entitlement of the People, not to mention the parties to the case, to full disclosure of the Court's reasons for what it decides. The notion that the so-called counter-majoritarian branch of the government need not tell all the reasons or the "real" reasons for its decision is a form of secrecy that offends democracy. It is not the same as the constructive privacy that surrounds the deliberative process between oral argument and the public announcement of a decision.

In Our aspiration to be an intelligent democracy governed by the rule of law, the Court has an even greater obligation than the president and Congress to speak with candor and with clarity. The justices are not subject to periodic review by election. Except for the processes of amendment, they have the last word on what the Constitution requires, prohibits, and permits. When they do not speak with candor and clarity in their opinions, they deprive Us, the governed, of the capacity to know what the law does and does not re-

quire, and thus exclude Us from the opportunity to
participate fully in government. Likewise, they deprive the governors (who are also counted among the
governed) of guidelines for meeting their constitutional
responsibilities. "For disclosure, absence of deception,
almost defines," as Professor Vining makes clear,
"what it means to be *inside* rather than *outside* an
entity."[17] This canon, like the first, seeks to make the
Court more sensitive than it seems sometimes to be to
its obligations to inform the People directly—to see to
it that We remain insiders.

3. *Acknowledge and explain deliberate ambiguity.*

This canon recognizes, as did Chief Justice Marshall
in *McCulloch*, that such are the frailties of human language and human perception "that no word conveys to
the mind, in all situations, one single definite idea."[18]
But it also recognizes that some phrases and words are
clearer than others, and it expresses a strong preference for avoiding the use of those that are more rather
than less ambiguous. Within the margins of unavoidable
ambiguity, the Court's opinion-writing task is, after all,
to give understanding to language of the Constitution
that has conveyed different meanings to different minds
at different times.

This canon also acknowledges and accepts that for
an opinion to gain the support of a majority and thus
to speak with the authority of the Court, "compromise
in the form of ambiguity may [sometimes] be inevita-

ble."[19] It takes into account Justice Stone's explanation of why in *Educational Films Corp. v. Ward*[20] he
did not write an "unambiguous" opinion of the Court
like that proposed as an alternative by T. R. Powell in
his article "An Imaginary Judicial Opinion."[21] In a
letter to Professor Powell, the Justice wrote:

> I should have preferred to have written your opinion than
> the one which will actually appear in the books. Had I
> done so, I should have been in a minority of two or three,
> instead of a majority of six. Someone else would have
> written the opinion and, I fear, would have said some
> approving words (which I carefully avoided in this and
> other cases) of doctrine, about which the less said the
> better, unless it be flatly disapproved. In other words, you
> will see that I proceed upon the theory, which I am
> willing to admit may be a mistaken one, that the large
> objective should be kept constantly in mind and reached
> by whatever road is open, provided only that untenable
> distinctions are not taken, and that I am not, in the pro-
> cess, committed incidentally to the doctrine of which I
> disapprove or which would hinder the Court's coming out
> ultimately in the right place.[22]

To accept as a given the forces for compromise in the
opinion-writing environment described by Justice
Stone is not to suggest, and he does not, that the Court
is thereby relieved of its responsibility to speak with
candor in language that We can understand.

Candor requires that ambiguity be unambiguously
acknowledged. In appropriate cases, the majority opinion should explain, for example, that it has been unable

to find or fashion a clearly graspable principle or set
of reasons on which to rest its judgment. This canon
thus recognizes the continuing nature of the process
by which Supreme Court justices develop constitutional doctrine. "They grapple," as Professor Rostow
has observed, "with a new problem, deal with it over
and over again, as its dimensions change.... They back
and fill, zig and zag, groping through the mist for a line
of thought which will in the end satisfy their standards
of craft."[23] The justices can, as they zig and zag, deal
forthrightly with ambiguity by acknowledging the extent of their differences in unanimity bought by compromise and in division evidenced by majority,
concurring, and dissenting opinions.

   This canon rejects the notion that deliberate ambiguity need not be acknowledged. It questions, for
example, the way in which Chief Justice Charles Evans
Hughes dealt with the inclusion of incompatible views.
He is reported to have said that "he tried to write his
opinions clearly and logically, but if he needed the fifth
vote of a colleague who insisted on putting in a paragraph that did not 'belong,' in it went, and let the law
reviews figure out what it meant."[24] To leave the task
of discovering and explaining the intended ambiguity
to specialists, who write in a jargon-bound language to
one another in journals of limited circulation, is to
breach the Court's obligation to write so as to enable
the People to figure out what it did and did not mean
to say about the Constitution. Bargaining for votes neither justifies nor makes inevitable the Court's aban-

donment of its task to disclose and explain when the majority is uncertain about the reasons for its decision.

The purpose of this canon is to make visible the basis, however limited, on which the judgment that the justices share is reached in the opinion that they join. Deliberately ambiguous opinions can then be written in good faith and be taken seriously as the Court continually seeks to refine the reasons behind the constitutional law it articulates.

4. *Be accurate and scrupulously fair in making attributions to another opinion in the case.*

This canon recognizes that concurrences and dissents are meant to disclose and clarify important differences within the Court. It recognizes that all the opinions in a case ought to constitute a single communication and that therefore the justices have a common obligation to give fair and accurate readings to the views of their colleagues that they challenge or share. The canon is aimed at avoiding making ambiguous that which is not and at discouraging the distortion of another's opinion in order to score a debater's point. Justice Jackson has observed, "The technique of the dissenter often is to exaggerate the holding of the Court beyond the meaning of the majority and then to blast away at the excess. So the poor lawyer with a similar case does not know whether the majority opinion meant what it seemed to say or what the minority said it meant."[25] Such exaggeration must not be indulged in if the Court is to make accessible, not only to the poor lawyer, but to all of Us what it meant to say and what it did not mean to say. U.S. Court of Appeals Judge Frank M. Coffin put it this way, "If I am taking a position that differs from what I think one of my colleagues would prefer, I will...state his position as fairly and strongly in the opinion as I can and proceed to deal with it."[26]

This canon is not unrelated to those canons concerned with the use of understandable language, candor, and ambiguity. Its separate status, however, underscores the importance of assessing the Court's total work product in a case as a single communication. This is a requisite of taking differences within the Court seriously. Chief Justice Rehnquist has noted:

> It may well be that the nature of constitutional adjudication invites, at least, if it does not require, more separate opinions than does adjudication of issues of law in other areas....When reasonable minds may and do frequently disagree as to the proper interpretation of a constitutional provision, there is a natural tendency on the part of a justice to want to state his own views if they differ significantly from those of the majority of his brethren. A dissent in a constitutional case is not merely, as Chief Justice Hughes described..., an appeal to the brooding spirit of the law. It is an appeal to present and future brethren to see the light.[27]

This canon is designed to protect the integrity of each of the opinions in a constitutional case to ensure that their appeals are taken seriously in what Laurence

Tribe calls one of the higher values—"the open ventilation of conflicting views on the meaning of the Constitution, both as a way of engaging the nation in debate and as a way of modeling what such a debate at its best can be."[28]

5. Incorporate in the text, rather than relegate to footnotes, material that is directly related to the reasons for the decision or to the meaning or breadth of the holding.

This canon links the physical accessibility of the words in an opinion to its substantive accessibility to the general public. U.S. Court of Appeals Judge Abner J. Mikva, who has sworn off using footnotes in his opinions, has asserted:

> When reading a footnoted opinion one's eyes are constantly moving from text to footnotes and back again. The distraction and time waste are substantial. If [substantive] footnotes were a rational form of communication, Darwinian selection would have resulted in the eyes being set vertically rather than on an inefficient horizontal plane.[29]

The footnote thus separates the opinion from the general public. It inserts the professional reader between the Court and the People.

This canon addresses a problem not dealt with directly in the opinion studies. It is aimed at making visible, rather than obscuring, the differences and agreements critical to understanding what the Court says and does not say about the Constitution.

Nixon v. Fitzgerald[30] provides a good example of the need for this canon and of why footnotes are frequently "the most eagerly studied parts of Supreme Court opinions."[31] The opinion of the Court, delivered by Justice Powell and joined by four others, held that "a former President of the United States ... is entitled to absolute immunity from [civil] damages liability predicated on his official acts."[32] It explained that the president's absolute immunity is "a functionally mandated incident of [his] unique office rooted in the constitutional tradition of the separation of powers."[33] At the same time, the Court closed a long footnote—number twenty-seven—with: "[O]ur holding today need only be that the President is absolutely immune from civil damages liability for his official acts in the absence of explicit affirmative action by Congress. We decide only this constitutional issue, which is necessary to disposition of the case before us."[34]

Chief Justice Burger, who joined the Court's opinion, wrote separately "to underscore that the Presidential immunity derives from and is mandated by the constitutional doctrine of separation of powers."[35] In the final paragraph of his concurrence, he reiterated "that the constitutional concept of separation of independent coequal powers dictates that a President be immune from civil damages actions based on acts within the scope of Executive authority while in office."[36] To that sentence, the Chief Justice attached a

footnote in which he challenged footnote twenty-seven
of the opinion of the Court, which he joined. "The
Court," he wrote, as if his vote were not essential to
the majority,

> suggests that "we need not address directly" whether Con-
> gress could create a damages action against a President.
> However, the Court's holding, in my view, effectively re-
> solves that issue; once it is established that the Consti-
> tution confers absolute immunity, as the Court holds
> today, legislative action cannot alter that result. Nothing
> in the Court's opinion is to be read as suggesting that a
> constitutional holding of this Court can be legislatively
> overruled or modified.[37]

Justice White, in a dissenting opinion joined by Justices Brennan, Marshall, and Blackmun, added to these
text and subtext deliberations about the meaning of
absolute immunity. In his footnote thirty-seven, he
wrote, "THE CHIEF JUSTICE leaves no doubt that he, at
least, reads the majority opinion as standing for the
broad proposition that the President is absolutely immune under the Constitution."[38] And Justice White
added in the same footnote, "Similarly, THE CHIEF JUS-
TICE dismisses the majority's claim that it has not decided the question of whether Congress could create a
damages action against the President."[39] The footnote
accompanies text that does not seem to express these
reservations as to the meaning of the majority view:
"In the end, the majority seems to overcome its initial
hesitation for it announces that '[w]e consider [abso-

lute] immunity a functionally mandated incident of the President's unique office.' "[40]

To recite this exchange between text and subtext in *Nixon v. Fitzgerald* within and among the sixty-six pages of opinions with eighty-nine footnotes is to demonstrate what this canon is meant to prevent.

With regard to what Judge Mikva calls *obiter dictum* ("by the way") footnotes, he has observed that they make the work of the Court less clear than it need be—incomprehensible, in fact, to the nonspecialists among Us: "As the footnotes and their unnecessary-to-the-opinion subject matter proliferate, so do the pages of the opinions. Point-counterpoint, countered-counterpoint—the majority and dissenters hurl footnotes at each other, sometimes becoming so provocative as to require answers in the body of the opinion itself."[41] This canon is thus designed to reduce one of the Court's style barriers to comprehensibility and to increase accessibility of the opinion-writer's ideas to the reader.

The justices, I suppose, would have little quarrel with these canons of comprehensibility. If they were to self-consciously fashion and to adopt something like them, the question then becomes how might the Court make them operational in the opinion-writing enterprise.

II

Following oral argument in each case, the justices confer together to exchange views, to cast tentative votes, and to make and accept opinion-writing assignments. What happens in the interval between this conference and the announcement of the Court's decision in a case is crucial. Yet no provision is made for the justices to come together again to review the final drafts of all the opinions in the case—the outcome of their efforts—before making them public.

A final-phase conference, like the initial case conference, would bring the nine justices together in a confidential setting without their staffs. Chief Justice Rehnquist has noted that

> the tradition of having only the justices themselves present at the Court's conference is a salutary one.... Its principal effect is to implement the observations of Justice Brandeis...that the Supreme Court is respected because "we do our own work." If a justice is to participate meaningfully in the conference, the justice must himself know the issues to be discussed.[42]

Indeed, a final-review conference free of law clerks might help to facilitate that goal and mitigate some of the untoward effects on opinion-writing of the bureaucratization of the Court. With regard to the dramatic increase in the number of clerks serving each justice, Professor Vining has observed that

> opinions too often seem things written by no one at all: they are very long, much too long to be written by judges struggling with an enormous increase in caseload: they are tyings of patchwork which seem, on their face, to express the institutional process of their making rather

than the thinking, feeling, and reasoning of the author and those persuaded with him....

And he suggests that the "court is no longer nine judges in dialogue with one another, trying to come to common ground and setting out in writing their agreements and disagreements with a special sense of the representative quality of their thinking...."[43] The final conference would seek to restore that dialogue. Its purpose would be to provide the justices with a regular occasion to assess the written opinion or set of written opinions in terms of their canons of comprehensibility. The conference (or some other means for review that the justices might choose) should provide an opportunity to fine-tune the opinions so that, whether read separately or together, they constitute a comprehensible contribution to understanding the Constitution.

Guided by these canons, a justice might begin a final-phase review by saying, for example, in:

1. *National League of Cities*. We need to deal with the ambiguity in the Court's opinion as reflected in Justice Blackmun's concurrence. His doubt about whether the opinion of the four justices he joins adopts a "balancing approach" can and ought to be resolved. Otherwise, it is not clear that we have an opinion of the Court.

2. *Garcia*. The dissenting opinions create unnecessary confusion about what the dissenters say and mean regarding *stare decisis*. Two of the four justices

who join Justice Powell's opinion write separately. Their dissents contradict views that, by joining the Powell opinion, they claimed to share. Justice Powell seems to exacerbate the confusion concerning *stare decisis* by joining one of the separate dissents. Otherwise, the Powell opinion for the dissenters, as well as the Blackmun opinion for the Court, seem to meet our canons of comprehensibility.

3. *Cooper.* Candor and the need to minimize ambiguity require that we acknowledge and explain the reasons for our decision to use the language of "desegregation" rather than that of "integration" in affirming the lower court order to enforce the "integration" plan for the Little Rock school system.

4. *Brown II.* Candor and clarity require that we try to explain how something we unanimously held unconstitutional in *Brown I* and *Bolling* may at the same time constitutionally be allowed to continue. We should openly acknowledge that we are waiving the constitutional rights of the schoolchildren in these cases for an indefinite period. We need to be more explicit about the equitable principles we want the lower courts to apply and, more specifically, what weight, if any, they are to give to the "clean hands" doctrine when fashioning the remedy in states that have observed only the "separate" prong of *Plessy*'s "separate and equal" reading of the Equal Protection Clause.

5. *Bakke.* We ought not to release this decision until the "central meaning" statement more accurately

reflects what the Court has decided, or until Justice
Powell explicitly observes in the text of his opinion that
Justice Brennan's "central meaning" statement attributes to his opinion what he does not say and does not
mean to imply.

Seeing We the People as the Court's primary au-
dience, the justices, whether or not in agreement with
an opinion, would assist its author's effort to use accessible prose for expounding the pertinent constitutional provisions. Their task would be to ensure the
integrity of each opinion, be it their own or that of a
colleague.

Convening the justices to work together without
staff would free them to review for the first and only
time in the decision-making process the work product
of the entire Court expounding the Constitution. The
conference's goal would be not to homogenize or blur
the substantive differences between the justices or to
exaggerate the areas of agreement. It would be to enhance their own communication, and hence Our understanding, of what the Court has and has not decided
and of which of its reasons are shared and which are
in dispute.

A pre-release review of the completed opinion(s)
in a constitutional law case is not designed, as was
Henry Hart's much discussed 1959 proposal in the *Harvard Law Review*, to provide more time for the "ma-
turing of collective thought" among the justices.[44]

Professor Hart intended to promote more substantial majorities or unanimity on the Court. Under my proposal, efforts to persuade, to find a compromise, and to change a view would be laid aside. Of course, votes might change and dissenters might become a majority and the majority turn into dissenters in a case, such as *National League of Cities*, if a Justice Blackmun were to discover that his vote was based on a misreading of the opinion he had joined. The suggestion here, however, is to leave undisturbed the alignment reached during the opinion-drafting phase. The justices would not address the substantive issues with which they had been grappling in their individual writings, and in their individual decisions to join or not to join the opinion of another. The conference would provide members of the Court with a focused opportunity to review together one another's work. It would be an occasion for meeting their institutional responsibility to ensure that the totality of opinions is comprehensible before the Court goes public.[45]*

---

*Something like a final conference appears to have been convened prior to the publication of the Court's opinion in *Cooper v. Aaron*. As was discussed in Chapter 3, the Court quickly announced its unanimous decision in that case, postponing for later the issuance of an opinion. According to Hutchinson, Justice Burton noted in his diary on September 29, 1958, the day when the Court announced its decision: "Nothing was said about any separate opinion/s [to] follow, but we expect one to [be] filed by Frankfurter, who joins the Court's opinion but wants to say something more. We were unable to dissuade him but did succeed in getting him not to announce it from the bench today." Hutchinson, Unanimity and Desegregation: Decisionmaking in the Supreme Court, 1948–1958, 68 *Geo. L.J.* 1, 82–83 (1979).

On October 3, 1958, Justice Frankfurter circulated a draft of his con-

An important task of the final-phase conference, as the canons suggest, would be to encourage the justices to deal with their different views openly. "Completed" opinions in which they ignore their differences and write past one another, or misstate or relegate these differences to a subtext of footnoted debates, would be corrected. The aim would be to achieve candor—to avoid the appearance of certainty and agreement when it does not exist.[46] To enhance Our understanding of the "richness and complexity" of constitutional principles, the justices would seek clarity without inflexibility.[47] Not unlike the actual provisions of the Constitution, constitutional principles fashioned by the Court should be kept, as Justice Harlan observed, "flex-

---

curring opinion. "The Court," wrote Hutchinson, "met in conference on Monday, October 6, the first day of the October 1958 Term, to discuss Frankfurter's plan to file his opinion. Two members of the Court, Black and Brennan, declared that if Frankfurter persisted, they would file a statement dissenting from his filing. The good humor of Mr. Justice Harlan helped to avoid a divisive public exchange. When Black and Brennan proposed their dissenting statement, Harlan distributed his own statement." It read, as reproduced by Hutchinson: "MR. JUSTICE HARLAN concurring in part, expressing a *dubitante* in part, and dissenting in part.

"I concur in the Court's opinion, filed September 29, 1958, in which I have already concurred. I doubt the wisdom of my Brother FRANKFURTER filing his separate opinion, but since I am unable to find any material difference between that opinion and the Court's opinion—and am confirmed in my reading of the former by my Brother FRANKFURTER'S express reaffirmation of the latter—I am content to leave his course of action to his own good judgment. I dissent from the action of my other Brethren in filing their separate opinion, believing that it is always a mistake to make a mountain out of a molehill. *Requiescat in pace*."

Hutchinson concluded: "Harlan's draft statement apparently helped to defuse the disagreement. Frankfurter filed his opinion that morning, but it was not announced from the bench; no other statements were published."

ible in [their] ability to respond to the endless mutations of fact presented."[48]

I have no blueprint for the Court. I limit myself to a few speculations about how such pre-release reviews, whether by conference or by some other means, might take root. The justices would draw on a collective sense of pride in the Court's work. The appeal would be to each justice's sense of self as author—or as a joiner—of an opinion. The signed opinions of justices are, after all, the primary record by which history will judge them.[49] They would be motivated by their sense of craft, by their wish to deliver opinions that are taken seriously, by their commitment to the Court as an institution, and by their sense of responsibility to We the People. Professor Paul A. Freund conveys the quality of such pride in his description of the writings of Justice Louis D. Brandeis:

> In considering these papers...as a study in the art of opinion-writing, it is easy to see, therefore, why the sense of craftsmanship was so deeply respected and cultivated by the Justice. More than a matter of style was involved; it was, at the risk of putting it pretentiously, a matter of morality. The opportunity to reach a multitude of minds from the eminence of the judicial office imposed its corresponding obligations, to plumb a problem to its depths, to sheath a hard-won judgment in the toughest fiber, to shun the facile and shoddy argument as a sin against the power of communication.[50]

This appeal to the many facets of pride that individual justices have in their own work as a part of the

Court's work is, no doubt, more easily invoked than fulfilled. As Judge Coffin has observed: "Any substantial criticism of one's best efforts cannot fail to assault one's pride. Fortunately, a bit of time sees the anguish pass and I am able to think constructively about the criticism, avoiding a posture of either haughty rejection or servile acceptance."[51] For John Marshall Harlan an important, though unnoted, role to be played by each justice is to improve the quality of all the opinions in a case. "[Harlan's] pride in the Court's work," we are told, "took precedence over personal recognition."[52]

One mark of professional jurists is their ability to recognize hurt to personal pride and to turn its force toward improving the quality of their opinions as well as the opinions of colleagues.[53] The desire for personal recognition need not undermine the institutional and professional obligation of the justices to make suggestions in a straightforward and constructive manner to improve the quality of opinions with which they disagree.

However, the justices, like many of us, may sometimes blind themselves and one another to when they are being less than candid, less than forthright in their collaborative enterprise. The final review is intended to make it easier for the Court to uncover and correct such problems.

Were the Court to establish a final-phase conference and were the justices to develop and become accustomed to observing their canons, the process might ultimately become obsolete, or at any rate dormant.

With or without a final review, if the Court were to develop canons of comprehensibility, and if the justices were to take seriously one another's efforts to help them abide by these canons, they would enhance their ability to expound without forgetting that it is the Constitution they are explaining to and on behalf of We the People who are sovereign.

I close this chapter and this book by repeating some closing words from the opening chapter:

> That the Constitution be intelligible and accessible to We the People of the United States is requisite to a government by consent; a government that guarantees equal protection and due process of law; a government that provides both the governed and the governors with a peaceful process for resolving conflicts about the Constitution's meaning, particularly with regard to individual rights. To make this observation is to recognize that the principles the Court develops, like the provisions of the Constitution, will always need interpretation. This is so because of the nature of words and because justices of the Court are no more capable than were the Framers at the Constitutional Convention of foreseeing future exigencies—particularly in settings in which one constitutional principle may come into conflict with another.

APPENDIX

THE CONSTITUTION OF THE UNITED STATES

We the People of the United States, in Order to form a more perfect Union, establish Justice, insure domestic Tranquility, provide for the common defence, promote the general Welfare, and secure the Blessings of Liberty to ourselves and our Posterity, do ordain and establish this Constitution for the United States of America.

ARTICLE I

SECTION 1. All legislative Powers herein granted shall be vested in a Congress of the United States, which shall consist of a Senate and House of Representatives.

SECTION 2. [1] The House of Representatives shall be composed of Members chosen every second Year by the People of the several States, and the Electors in each State shall have the Qualifications requisite for Electors of the most numerous Branch of the State Legislature.

[2] No Person shall be a Representative who shall not have attained to the Age of twenty five Years, and been seven Years a Citizen of the United States, and who shall not, when elected, be an Inhabitant of that State in which he shall be chosen.

[3] Representatives and direct [Taxes]* shall be apportioned among the several States which may be included within this Union, according to their respective Numbers[, which shall be determined by adding to the whole Number of free Persons, including those bound to Service for a Term of Years, and excluding Indians not taxed, three fifths of all other Persons].† The actual Enumeration shall be made within three Years after the first Meeting of the Congress of the United States, and within every subsequent Term of ten Years, in such Manner as they shall by Law direct. The Number of Representatives shall not exceed one for every thirty Thousand, but each State shall have at Least one Representative; and until such enumeration shall be made, the State of New Hampshire shall be entitled to chuse three, Massachusetts eight, Rhode Island and Providence Plantations one, Connecticut five, New York six, New Jersey four, Pennsylvania eight, Delaware one, Maryland six, Virginia ten, North Carolina five, South Carolina five, and Georgia three.

[4] When vacancies happen in the Representation from any State, the Executive Authority thereof shall issue Writs of Election to fill such Vacancies.

[5] The House of Representatives shall chuse their Speaker and other Officers; and shall have the sole Power of Impeachment.

SECTION 3. [1] The Senate of the United States shall be composed of two Senators from each State, [chosen by the Legislature thereof,]‡ for six Years; and each Senator shall have one Vote.

[2] Immediately after they shall be assembled in Consequence of the first Election, they shall be divided as equally as may be into three Classes. The Seats of the Senators of the first Class shall be

*See Amendment XVI.
†See Amendment XIV.
‡See Amendment XVII.

vacated at the Expiration of the second Year, of the second Class at the Expiration of the fourth Year, and of the third Class at the Expiration of the sixth Year, so that one third may be chosen every second Year[; and if Vacancies happen by Resignation, or otherwise, during the Recess of the Legislature of any State, the Executive thereof may make temporary Appointments until the next Meeting of the Legislature, which shall then fill such Vacancies].*

[3] No Person shall be a Senator who shall not have attained to the Age of thirty Years, and been nine Years a Citizen of the United States, and who shall not, when elected, be an Inhabitant of that State for which he shall be chosen.

[4] The Vice President of the United States shall be President of the Senate, but shall have no Vote, unless they be equally divided.

[5] The Senate shall chuse their other Officers, and also a President pro tempore, in the absence of the Vice President, or when he shall exercise the Office of President of the United States.

[6] The Senate shall have the sole Power to try all Impeachments. When sitting for that Purpose, they shall be on Oath or Affirmation. When the President of the United States is tried, the Chief Justice shall preside: And no Person shall be convicted without the Concurrence of two thirds of the Members present.

[7] Judgment in Cases of Impeachment shall not extend further than to removal from Office, and disqualification to hold and enjoy any Office of honor, Trust or Profit under the United States: but the Party convicted shall nevertheless be liable and subject to Indictment, Trial, Judgment and Punishment, according to Law.

SECTION 4. [1] The Times, Places and Manner of holding Elections for Senators and Representatives, shall be prescribed in each State by the Legislature thereof; but the Congress may at any time by Law make or alter such Regulations, except as to the Places of chusing Senators.

[[2] The Congress shall assemble at least once in every Year,

---

*See Amendment XVII.

and such Meeting shall be on the first Monday in December, unless they shall by Law appoint a different Day.]*

SECTION 5. [1] Each House shall be the Judge of the Elections, Returns and Qualifications of its own Members, and a Majority of each shall constitute a Quorum to do Business; but a smaller Number may adjourn from day to day, and may be authorized to compel the Attendance of absent Members, in such Manner, and under such Penalties as each House may provide.

[2] Each House may determine the Rules of its Proceedings, punish its Members for disorderly Behaviour, and, with the Concurrence of two thirds, expel a Member.

[3] Each House shall keep a Journal of its Proceedings, and from time to time publish the same, excepting such Parts as may in their Judgment require Secrecy; and the Yeas and Nays of the Members of either House on any question shall, at the Desire of one fifth of those Present, be entered on the Journal.

[4] Neither House, during the Session of Congress, shall, without the Consent of the other, adjourn for more than three days, nor to any other Place than that in which the two Houses shall be sitting.

SECTION 6. [1] The Senators and Representatives shall receive a Compensation for their Services, to be ascertained by Law, and paid out of the Treasury of the United States. They shall in all Cases, except Treason, Felony and Breach of the Peace, be privileged from Arrest during their Attendance at the Session of their respective Houses, and in going to and returning from the same; and for any Speech or Debate in either House, they shall not be questioned in any other Place.

[2] No Senator or Representative shall, during the Time for which he was elected, be appointed to any civil Office under the Authority of the United States, which shall have been created, or the Emoluments whereof shall have been encreased during such time; and no Person holding any Office under the United

*See Amendment XX.

States, shall be a Member of either House during his Continuance in Office.

SECTION 7. [1] All Bills for raising Revenue shall originate in the House of Representatives; but the Senate may propose or concur with Amendments as on other Bills.

[2] Every Bill which shall have passed the House of Representatives and the Senate, shall, before it become a Law, be presented to the President of the United States; If he approve he shall sign it, but if not he shall return it, with his Objections to the House in which it shall have originated, who shall enter the Objections at large on their Journal, and proceed to reconsider it. If after such Reconsideration two thirds of that House shall agree to pass the Bill, it shall be sent, together with the Objections, to the other House, by which it shall likewise be reconsidered, and if approved by two thirds of that House, it shall become a Law. But in all such Cases the Votes of both Houses shall be determined by Yeas and Nays, and the Names of the Persons voting for and against the Bill shall be entered on the Journal of each House respectively. If any Bill shall not be returned by the President within ten Days (Sundays excepted) after it shall have been presented to him, the Same shall be a Law, in like Manner as if he had signed it, unless the Congress by their Adjournment prevents its Return, in which Case it shall not be a Law.

[3] Every Order, Resolution, or Vote to which the Concurrence of the Senate and House of Representatives may be necessary (except on a question of Adjournment) shall be presented to the President of the United States; and before the Same shall take Effect, shall be approved by him, or being disapproved by him, shall be repassed by two thirds of the Senate and House of Representatives, according to the Rules and Limitations prescribed in the Case of a Bill.

SECTION 8. [1] The Congress shall have Power To lay and collect Taxes, Duties, Imposts and Excises, to pay the Debts and provide for the common Defence and general Welfare of the United

States; but all Duties, Imposts and Excises shall be uniform throughout the United States;

[2] To borrow money on the credit of the United States;

[3] To regulate Commerce with foreign Nations, and among the several States, and with the Indian Tribes;

[4] To establish an uniform Rule of Naturalization, and uniform Laws on the subject of Bankruptcies throughout the United States;

[5] To coin Money, regulate the Value thereof, and of foreign Coin, and fix the Standard of Weights and Measures;

[6] To provide the Punishment of counterfeiting the Securities and current Coin of the United States;

[7] To establish Post Offices and post Roads;

[8] To promote the Progress of Science and useful Arts, by securing for limited Times to Authors and Inventors the exclusive Right to their respective Writings and Discoveries;

[9] To constitute Tribunals inferior to the supreme Court;

[10] To define and punish Piracies and Felonies committed on the high Seas, and Offenses against the Law of Nations;

[11] To declare War, grant Letters of Marque and Reprisal, and make Rules concerning Captures on Land and Water;

[12] To raise and support Armies, but no Appropriation of Money to that Use shall be for a longer Term than two Years;

[13] To provide and maintain a Navy;

[14] To make Rules for the Government and Regulation of the land and naval Forces;

[15] To provide for calling forth the Militia to execute the Laws of the Union, suppress Insurrections and repel Invasions;

[16] To provide for organizing, arming, and disciplining, the Militia, and for governing such Part of them as may be employed in the Service of the United States, reserving to the States respectively, the Appointment of the Officers, and the Authority of training the Militia according to the discipline prescribed by Congress;

[17] To exercise exclusive Legislation in all Cases whatsoever, over such District (not exceeding ten Miles square) as may, by

Cession of particular States, and the Acceptance of Congress, become the Seat of the Government of the United States, and to exercise like Authority over all Places purchased by the Consent of the Legislature of the State in which the Same shall be, for the Erection of Forts, Magazines, Arsenals, dock-Yards, and other needful Buildings;—And

[18] To make all Laws which shall be necessary and proper for carrying into Execution the foregoing Powers, and all other Powers vested by this Constitution in the Government of the United States, or in any Department or Officer thereof.

SECTION 9. [1] The Migration or Importation of such Persons as any of the States now existing shall think proper to admit, shall not be prohibited by the Congress prior to the Year one thousand eight hundred and eight, but a Tax or duty may be imposed on such Importation, not exceeding ten dollars for each Person.

[2] The privilege of the Writ of Habeas Corpus shall not be suspended, unless when in Cases of Rebellion or Invasion the public Safety may require it.

[3] No Bill of Attainder or ex post facto Law shall be passed.

[[4] No Capitation, or other direct, Tax shall be laid, unless in Proportion to the Census or Enumeration herein before directed to be taken.]*

[5] No Tax or Duty shall be laid on Articles exported from any State.

[6] No Preference shall be given by any Regulation of Commerce or Revenue to the Ports of one State over those of another; nor shall Vessels bound to, or from, one State, be obliged to enter, clear, or pay Duties in another.

[7] No Money shall be drawn from the Treasury, but in Consequence of Appropriations made by Law; and a regular Statement and Account of the Receipts and Expenditures of all public Money shall be published from time to time.

[8] No Title of Nobility shall be granted by the United States:

*See Amendment XVI.

And no Person holding any Office of Profit or Trust under them, shall, without the Consent of the Congress, accept of any present, Emolument, Office, or Title, of any kind whatever, from any King, Prince, or foreign State.

SECTION 10. [1] No State shall enter into any Treaty, Alliance, or Confederation; grant Letters of Marque and Reprisal; coin Money; emit Bills of Credit; make any Thing but gold and silver Coin a Tender in Payment of Debts; pass any Bill of Attainder, ex post facto Law, or Law impairing the Obligation of Contracts, or grant any Title of Nobility.

[2] No State shall, without the Consent of the Congress, lay any Imposts or Duties on Imports or Exports, except what may be absolutely necessary for executing its inspection Laws: and the net Produce of all Duties and Imposts, laid by any State on Imports or Exports, shall be for the Use of the Treasury of the United States; and all such Laws shall be subject to the Revision and Controul of the Congress.

[3] No State shall, without the Consent of Congress, lay any Duty of Tonnage, keep Troops, or Ships of War in time of Peace, enter into any Agreement or Compact with another State, or with a foreign Power, or engage in War, unless actually invaded, or in such imminent Danger as will not admit of delay.

ARTICLE II

SECTION 1. [1] The executive Power shall be vested in a President of the United States of America. He shall hold his Office during the Term of four Years, and, together with the Vice President, chosen for the same Term, be elected, as follows:

[2] Each State shall appoint, in such Manner as the Legislature thereof may direct, a Number of Electors, equal to the whole Number of Senators and Representatives to which the State may be entitled in the Congress: but no Senator or Representative, or Per-

son holding an Office of Trust or Profit under the United States, shall be appointed an Elector.

[[3] The Electors shall meet in their respective States, and vote by Ballot for two Persons, of whom one at least shall not be an Inhabitant of the same State with themselves. And they shall make a List of all the Persons voted for, and of the Number of Votes for each; which List they shall sign and certify, and transmit sealed to the Seat of the Government of the United States, directed to the President of the Senate. The President of the Senate shall, in the Presence of the Senate and House of Representatives, open all the Certificates, and the Votes shall then be counted. The Person having the greatest Number of Votes shall be the President, if such Number be a Majority of the whole Number of Electors appointed; and if there be more than one who have such Majority, and have an equal Number of Votes, then the House of Representatives shall immediately chuse by Ballot one of them for President; and if no Person have a Majority, then from the five highest on the List the said House shall in like Manner chuse the President. But in chusing the President, the Votes shall be taken by States, the Representation from each State having one Vote; a quorum for this Purpose shall consist of a Member or Members from two thirds of the States, and a Majority of all the States shall be necessary to a Choice. In every Case, after the Choice of the President, the Person having the greatest Number of Votes of the Electors shall be the Vice President. But if there should remain two or more who have equal Votes, the Senate shall chuse from them by Ballot the Vice President.]*

[4] The Congress may determine the Time of chusing the Electors, and the Day on which they shall give their Votes; which Day shall be the same throughout the United States.

[5] No person except a natural born Citizen, or a Citizen of the United States, at the time of the Adoption of this Constitution, shall be eligible to the Office of President; neither shall any Person be

*See Amendment XII.

eligible to that Office who shall not have attained to the Age of thirty five Years, and been fourteen years a Resident within the United States.

[[6] In Case of the removal of the President from Office, or of his Death, Resignation, or Inability to discharge the Powers and Duties of the said Office, the Same shall devolve on the Vice President, and the Congress may by law provide for the Case of Removal, Death, Resignation or Inability, both of the President and Vice President, declaring what Officer shall then act as President, and such Officer shall act accordingly, until the Disability be removed, or a President shall be elected.]*

[7] The President shall, at stated Times, receive for his Services, a Compensation, which shall neither be increased nor diminished during the Period for which he shall have been elected, and he shall not receive within that Period any other Emolument from the United States, or any of them.

[8] Before he enter on the Execution of his Office, he shall take the following oath or Affirmation: "I do solemnly swear (or affirm) that I will faithfully execute the Office of President of the United States, and will to the best of my Ability, preserve, protect and defend the Constitution of the United States."

SECTION 2. [1] The President shall be Commander in Chief of the Army and Navy of the United States, and of the Militia of the several States, when called into the actual Service of the United States; he may require the Opinion, in writing, of the principal Officer in each of the executive Departments, upon any Subject relating to the Duties of their respective Offices, and he shall have Power to grant Reprieves and Pardons for Offenses against the United States, except in Cases of Impeachment.

[2] He shall have Power, by and with the Advice and Consent of the Senate, to make Treaties, provided two thirds of the Senators present concur; and he shall nominate, and by and with the Advice and Consent of the Senate, shall appoint Ambassadors, other public

*See Amendment XXV.

Ministers and Consuls, Judges of the supreme Court, and all other Officers of the United States, whose Appointments are not herein otherwise provided for, and which shall be established by Law: but the Congress may by Law vest the Appointment of such inferior Officers, as they think proper, in the President alone, in the Courts of Law, or in the Heads of Departments.

[3] The President shall have Power to fill up all Vacancies that may happen during the Recess of the Senate, by granting Commissions which shall expire at the End of their next Session.

SECTION 3. He shall from time to time give to the Congress Information of the State of the Union, and recommend to their Consideration such Measures as he shall judge necessary and expedient; he may, on extraordinary Occasions, convene both Houses, or either of them, and in Case of Disagreement between them, with Respect to the Time of Adjournment, he may adjourn them to such Time as he shall think proper; he shall receive Ambassadors and other public Ministers; he shall take Care that the Laws be faithfully executed, and shall Commission all the Officers of the United States.

SECTION 4. The President, Vice President and all civil Officers of the United States, shall be removed from Office on Impeachment for, and Conviction of, Treason, Bribery, or other high Crimes and Misdemeanors.

ARTICLE III

SECTION 1. The judicial Power of the United States, shall be vested in one supreme Court, and in such inferior Courts as the Congress may from time to time ordain and establish. The Judges, both of the supreme and inferior Courts, shall hold their Offices during good Behaviour, and shall, at stated Times, receive for their Services, a Compensation, which shall not be diminished during their Continuance in Office.

SECTION 2. [1] The Judicial Power shall extend to all Cases, in Law and Equity, arising under this Constitution, the Laws of the United States, and Treaties made, or which shall be made, under their Authority;—to all Cases affecting Ambassadors, other public Ministers and Consuls;—to all Cases of admiralty and maritime Jurisdiction;—to Controversies to which the United States shall be a Party;—to Controversies between two or more States;[—between a State and Citizens of another State;]*—between Citizens of different States;—between Citizens of the same State claiming Lands under Grants of different States[, and between a State, or the Citizens thereof, and foreign States, Citizens or Subjects].†

[2] In all Cases affecting Ambassadors, other public Ministers and Consuls, and those in which a State shall be a Party, the supreme Court shall have original Jurisdiction. In all the other Cases before mentioned, the supreme Court shall have appellate Jurisdiction, both as to Law and Fact, with such Exceptions, and under such Regulations as the Congress shall make.

[3] The trial of all Crimes, except in Cases of Impeachment, shall be by Jury; and such Trial shall be held in the State where the said Crimes shall have been committed; but when not committed within any State, the Trial shall be at such Place or Places as the Congress may by Law have directed.

SECTION 3. [1] Treason against the United States, shall consist only in levying War against them, or in adhering to their Enemies, giving them Aid and Comfort. No Person shall be convicted of Treason unless on the Testimony of two Witnesses to the same overt Act, or on Confession in open Court.

[2] The Congress shall have Power to declare the Punishment of Treason, but no Attainder of Treason shall work Corruption of Blood, or Forfeiture except during the Life of the Person attainted.

*See Amendment XI.
†See Amendment XI.

ARTICLE IV

SECTION 1. Full Faith and Credit shall be given in each State to the public Acts, Records, and judicial Proceedings of every other State. And the Congress may by general Laws prescribe the Manner in which such Acts, Records and Proceedings shall be proved, and the Effect thereof.

SECTION 2. [1] The Citizens of each State shall be entitled to all Privileges and Immunities of Citizens in the several States.

[2] A Person charged in any State with Treason, Felony, or other Crime, who shall flee from Justice, and be found in another State, shall on demand of the executive Authority of the State from which he fled, be delivered up, to be removed to the State having Jurisdiction of the Crime.

[[3] No Person held to Service or Labour in one State, under the Laws thereof, escaping into another, shall, in Consequence of any Law or Regulation therein, be discharged from such Service or Labour, but shall be delivered up on Claim of the Party to whom such Service or Labour may be due.]*

SECTION 3. [1] New States may be admitted by the Congress into this Union; but no new State shall be formed or erected within the Jurisdiction of any other State; nor any State be formed by the Junction of two or more States, or Parts of States, without the Consent of the Legislatures of the States concerned as well as of the Congress.

[2] The Congress shall have Power to dispose of and make all needful Rules and Regulations respecting the Territory or other Property belonging to the United States; and nothing in this Constitution shall be so construed as to Prejudice any Claims of the United States, or of any particular State.

SECTION 4. The United States shall guarantee to every State in

*See Amendment XIII.

this Union a Republican Form of Government, and shall protect each of them against Invasion; and on Application of the Legislature, or of the Executive (when the Legislature cannot be convened) against domestic Violence.

ARTICLE V

The Congress, whenever two thirds of both Houses shall deem it necessary, shall propose Amendments to this Constitution, or, on the Application of the Legislatures of two thirds of the several States, shall call a Convention for proposing Amendments, which, in either Case, shall be valid to all Intents and Purposes, as part of this Constitution, when ratified by the Legislatures of three fourths of the several States, or by Conventions in three fourths thereof, as the one or the other Mode of Ratification may be proposed by the Congress; Provided that no Amendment which may be made prior to the Year One thousand eight hundred and eight shall in any Manner affect the first and fourth Clauses in the Ninth Section of the first Article; and that no State, without its Consent, shall be deprived of its equal Suffrage in the Senate.

ARTICLE VI

[1] All Debts contracted and Engagements entered into, before the Adoption of this Constitution, shall be as valid against the United States under this Constitution, as under the Confederation.

[2] This Constitution, and the Laws of the United States which shall be made in Pursuance thereof; and all Treaties made, or which shall be made, under the Authority of the United States, shall be the supreme Law of the Land; and the Judges in every State shall

be bound thereby, any Thing in the Constitution or Laws of any State to the Contrary notwithstanding.

[3] The Senators and Representatives before mentioned, and the Members of the several State Legislatures, and all executive and judicial Officers, both of the United States and of the several States, shall be bound by Oath or Affirmation, to support this Constitution; but no religious Test shall ever be required as a Qualification to any Office or public Trust under the United States.

ARTICLE VII

The Ratification of the Conventions of nine States shall be sufficient for the Establishment of this Constitution between the States so ratifying the Same.

Done in Convention by the Unanimous Consent of the States present the Seventeenth Day of September in the Year of our Lord one thousand seven hundred and Eighty seven and of the Independence of the United States of America the Twelfth.

ARTICLES IN ADDITION TO, AND AMENDMENT OF, THE CONSTITUTION OF THE UNITED STATES OF AMERICA, PROPOSED BY CONGRESS, AND RATIFIED BY THE LEGISLATURES OF THE SEVERAL STATES, PURSUANT TO THE FIFTH ARTICLE OF THE ORIGINAL CONSTITUTION

AMENDMENT I [1791]

Congress shall make no law respecting an establishment of religion, or prohibiting the free exercise thereof; or abridging the freedom of speech, or of the press; or the right of the people peaceably to assemble, and to petition the Government for a redress of grievances.

AMENDMENT II [1791]

A well regulated Militia, being necessary to the security of a free State, the right of the people to keep and bear Arms, shall not be infringed.

AMENDMENT III [1791]

No Soldier shall, in time of peace be quartered in any house, without the consent of the Owner, nor in time of war, but in a manner to be prescribed by law.

AMENDMENT IV [1791]

The right of the people to be secure in their persons, houses, papers, and effects, against unreasonable searches and seizures, shall not be violated, and no Warrants shall issue, but upon probable cause, supported by Oath or affirmation, and particularly describing the place to be searched, and the persons or things to be seized.

AMENDMENT V [1791]

No person shall be held to answer for a capital, or otherwise in-famous crime, unless on a presentment or indictment of a Grand Jury, except in cases arising in the land or naval forces, or in the

Militia, when in actual service in time of War or public danger; nor shall any person be subject for the same offence to be twice put in jeopardy of life or limb; nor shall be compelled in any criminal case to be a witness against himself, nor be deprived of life, liberty, or property, without due process of law; nor shall private property be taken for public use, without just compensation.

AMENDMENT VI [1791]

In all criminal prosecutions, the accused shall enjoy the right to a speedy and public trial, by an impartial jury of the State and district wherein the crime shall have been committed, which district shall have been previously ascertained by law, and to be informed of the nature and cause of the accusation; to be confronted with the witnesses against him; to have compulsory process for obtaining witnesses in his favor, and to have the Assistance of Counsel for his defence.

AMENDMENT VII [1791]

In Suits at common law, where the value in controversy shall exceed twenty dollars, the right of trial by jury shall be preserved, and no fact tried by a jury, shall be otherwise re-examined in any Court of the United States, than according to the rules of the common law.

AMENDMENT VIII [1791]

Excessive bail shall not be required, nor excessive fines imposed, nor cruel and unusual punishments inflicted.

AMENDMENT IX [1791]

The enumeration in the Constitution, of certain rights, shall not be construed to deny or disparage others retained by the people.

AMENDMENT X [1791]

The powers not delegated to the United States by the Constitution, nor prohibited by it to the States, are reserved to the States respectively, or to the people.

AMENDMENT XI [1798]

The Judicial power of the United States shall not be construed to extend to any suit in law or equity, commenced or prosecuted against one of the United States by Citizens of another State, or by Citizens or Subjects of any Foreign State.

AMENDMENT XII [1804]

The Electors shall meet in their respective states and vote by ballot for President and Vice-President, one of whom, at least, shall not be an inhabitant of the same state with themselves; they shall name in their ballots the person voted for as President, and in distinct ballots the person voted for as Vice-President, and they shall make distinct lists of all persons voted for as President, and of all persons voted for as Vice-President, and of the number of votes for each, which lists they shall sign and certify, and transmit sealed to the

seat of the government of the United States, directed to the President of the Senate;—The President of the Senate shall, in the
presence of the Senate and House of Representatives, open all the
certificates and the votes shall then be counted;—The person having
the greatest number of votes for President, shall be the President,
if such number be a majority of the whole number of Electors
appointed; and if no person have such majority, then from the
persons having the highest numbers not exceeding three on the list
of those voted for as President, the House of Representatives shall
choose immediately, by ballot, the President. But in choosing the
President, the votes shall be taken by states, the representation
from each state having one vote; a quorum for this purpose shall
consist of a member or members from two-thirds of the states, and
a majority of all the states shall be necessary to a choice. And if
the House of Representatives shall not choose a President whenever the right of choice shall devolve upon them, before the fourth
day of March next following, then the Vice-President shall act as
President, as in the case of the death or other constitutional disability of the President.—The person having the greatest number
of votes as Vice-President, shall be the Vice-President, if such
number be a majority of the whole number of Electors appointed,
and if no person have a majority, then from the two highest numbers
on the list, the Senate shall choose the Vice-President; a quorum
for the purpose shall consist of two-thirds of the whole number of
Senators, and a majority of the whole number shall be necessary
to a choice. But no person constitutionally ineligible to the office
of President shall be eligible to that of Vice-President of the United
States.

AMENDMENT XIII [1865]

SECTION 1. Neither slavery nor involuntary servitude, except as a
punishment for crime whereof the party shall have been duly con-

victed, shall exist within the United States, or any place subject to their jurisdiction.

SECTION 2. Congress shall have power to enforce this article by appropriate legislation.

AMENDMENT XIV [1868]

SECTION 1. All persons born or naturalized in the United States, and subject to the jurisdiction thereof, are citizens of the United States and of the State wherein they reside. No State shall make or enforce any law which shall abridge the privileges or immunities of citizens of the United States; nor shall any State deprive any person of life, liberty, or property, without due process of law; nor deny to any person within its jurisdiction the equal protection of the laws.

SECTION 2. Representatives shall be apportioned among the several States according to their respective numbers, counting the whole number of persons in each State, excluding Indians not taxed. But when the right to vote at any election for the choice of electors for President and Vice President of the United States, Representatives in Congress, the Executive and Judicial officers of a State, or the members of the Legislature thereof, is denied to any of the male inhabitants of such State, being twenty-one years of age, and citizens of the United States, or in any way abridged, except for participation in rebellion, or other crime, the basis of representation therein shall be reduced in the proportion which the number of such male citizens shall bear to the whole number of male citizens twenty-one years of age in such State.

SECTION 3. No person shall be a Senator or Representative in Congress, or elector of President and Vice President, or hold any office, civil or military, under the United States, or under any State, who, having previously taken an oath, as a member of Congress, or as an officer of the United States, or as a member of any State legislature, or as an executive or judicial officer of any State, to support the Constitution of the United States, shall have engaged in insurrection or rebellion against the same, or given aid or comfort to the enemies thereof. But Congress may by a vote of two-thirds of each House, remove such disability.

SECTION 4. The validity of the public debt of the United States, authorized by law, including debts incurred for payment of pensions and bounties for services in suppressing insurrection or rebellion, shall not be questioned. But neither the United States nor any State shall assume or pay any debt or obligation incurred in aid of insurrection or rebellion against the United States, or any claim for the loss of emancipation of any slave; but all such debts, obligations and claims shall be held illegal and void.

SECTION 5. The Congress shall have power to enforce, by appropriate legislation, the provisions of this article.

AMENDMENT XV [1870]

SECTION 1. The right of citizens of the United States to vote shall not be denied or abridged by the United States or by any State on account of race, color, or previous condition of servitude.

SECTION 2. The Congress shall have power to enforce this article by appropriate legislation.

AMENDMENT XVI [1913]

The Congress shall have power to lay and collect taxes on incomes, from whatever source derived, without apportionment among the several States, and without regard to any census or enumeration.

AMENDMENT XVII [1913]

[1] The Senate of the United States shall be composed of two Senators from each State, elected by the people thereof, for six years; and each Senator shall have one vote. The electors in each State shall have the qualifications requisite for electors of the most numerous branch of the State legislatures.

[2] When vacancies happen in the representation of any State in the Senate, the executive authority of such State shall issue writs of election to fill such vacancies: *Provided*, That the legislature of any State may empower the executive thereof to make temporary appointments until the people fill the vacancies by election as the legislature may direct.

[3] This amendment shall not be so construed as to affect the election or term of any Senator chosen before it becomes valid as part of the Constitution.

AMENDMENT XVIII [1919]

SECTION 1. After one year from the ratification of this article the manufacture, sale, or transportation of intoxicating liquors within, the importation thereof into, or the exportation thereof from the United States and all territory subject to the jurisdiction thereof for beverage purposes is hereby prohibited.

SECTION 2. The Congress and the several States shall have concurrent power to enforce this article by appropriate legislation.

SECTION 3. This article shall be inoperative unless it shall have been ratified as an amendment to the Constitution by the legislatures of the several States, as provided in the Constitution, within seven years from the date of the submission hereof to the States by the Congress.*

*See Amendment XXI.

AMENDMENT XIX [1920]

[1] The right of citizens of the United States to vote shall not be denied or abridged by the United States or by any State on account of sex.

[2] Congress shall have power to enforce this article by appropriate legislation.

AMENDMENT XX [1933]

SECTION 1. The terms of the President and Vice President shall end at noon on the 20th day of January, and the terms of Senators and Representatives at noon on the 3d day of January, of the years in which such terms would have ended if this article had not been ratified; and the terms of their successors shall then begin.

SECTION 2. The Congress shall assemble at least once in every year, and such meeting shall begin at noon on the 3d of January, unless they shall by law appoint a different day.

SECTION 3. If, at the time fixed for the beginning of the term of the President, the President elect shall have died, the Vice President elect shall become President. If a President shall not have been chosen before the time fixed for the beginning of his term, or if the President elect shall have failed to qualify, then the Vice President elect shall act as President until a President shall have qualified; and the Congress may by law provide for the case wherein neither a President elect nor a Vice President elect shall have qualified, declaring who shall then act as President, or the manner in which one who is to act shall be selected, and such person shall act accordingly until a President or Vice President shall have qualified.

SECTION 4. The Congress may by law provide for the case of the death of any of the persons from whom the House of Representatives may choose a President whenever the right of choice shall have devolved upon them, and for the case of the death of any of the persons from whom the Senate may choose a Vice President whenever the right of choice shall have devolved upon them.

SECTION 5. Sections 1 and 2 shall take effect on the 15th day of October following the ratification of this article.

SECTION 6. This article shall be inoperative unless it shall have been ratified as an amendment to the Constitution by the legislatures of three-fourths of the several States within seven years from the date of its submission.

AMENDMENT XXI [1933]

SECTION 1. The eighteenth article of amendment to the Constitution of the United States is hereby repealed.

SECTION 2. The transportation or importation into any State, Territory, or possession of the United States for delivery or use therein of intoxicating liquors, in violation of the laws thereof, is hereby prohibited.

SECTION 3. This article shall be inoperative unless it shall have been ratified as an amendment to the Constitution by conventions in the several States, as provided in the Constitution, within seven years from the date of the submission hereof to the States by the Congress.

AMENDMENT XXII [1951]

SECTION 1. No person shall be elected to the office of the President more than twice, and no person who has held the office of President, or acted as President, for more than two years of a term to which some other person was elected President shall be elected to the office of the President more than once. But this Article shall not apply to any person holding the office of President when this Article was proposed by the Congress, and shall not prevent any person who may be holding the office of President, or acting as President, during the term within which the Article becomes operative from holding the office of President or acting as President during the remainder of such term.

SECTION 2. This article shall be inoperative unless it shall have been ratified as an amendment to the Constitution by the legislatures of three-fourths of the several States within seven years from the date of its submission to the States by the Congress.

AMENDMENT XXIII [1961]

SECTION 1. The District constituting the seat of Government of the United States shall appoint in such manner as the Congress may direct:

A number of electors of President and Vice President equal to the whole number of Senators and Representatives in Congress to which the District would be entitled if it were a State, but in no event more than the least populous State; they shall be in addition to those appointed by the States, but they shall be considered, for the purposes of the election of President and Vice President, to be electors appointed by a State; and they shall meet in the District and perform such duties as provided by the twelfth article of amendment.

SECTION 2. The Congress shall have power to enforce this article by appropriate legislation.

AMENDMENT XXIV [1964]

SECTION 1. The right of citizens of the United States to vote in any primary or other election for President or Vice President, for electors for President or Vice President, or for Senator or Representative in Congress, shall not be denied or abridged by the United States or any State by reason of failure to pay any poll tax or other tax.

SECTION 2. The Congress shall have power to enforce this article by appropriate legislation.

AMENDMENT XXV [1967]

SECTION 1. In case of the removal of the President from office or of his death or resignation, the Vice President shall become President.

SECTION 2. Whenever there is a vacancy in the office of the Vice President, the President shall nominate a Vice President who shall take office upon confirmation by a majority vote of both Houses of Congress.

SECTION 3. Whenever the President transmits to the President pro tempore of the Senate and the Speaker of the House of Representatives his written declaration that he is unable to discharge the powers and duties of his office, and until he transmits to them a written declaration to the contrary, such powers and duties shall be discharged by the Vice President as Acting President.

SECTION 4. Whenever the Vice President and a majority of either the principal officers of the executive departments or of such other body as Congress may by law provide, transmit to the President pro tempore of the Senate and the Speaker of the House of Representatives their written declaration that the President is unable to discharge the powers and duties of his office, the Vice President shall immediately assume the powers and duties of the office as Acting President.

Thereafter, when the President transmits to the President pro tempore of the Senate and the Speaker of the House of Representatives his written declaration that no inability exists, he shall resume the powers and duties of his office unless the Vice President and a majority of either the principal officers of the executive department or of such other body as Congress may by law provide, transmit within four days to the President pro tempore of the Senate and the Speaker of the House of Representatives their written declaration that the President is unable to discharge the powers and duties of his office. Thereupon Congress shall decide the issue, assembling within forty-eight hours for that purpose if not in session. If the Congress, within twenty-one days after receipt of the latter written declaration, or, if Congress is not in session, within twenty-one days after Congress is required to assemble, determines by two-thirds vote of both Houses that the President is unable to discharge the powers and duties of his office, the Vice President shall continue to discharge the same as Acting President; otherwise, the President shall resume the powers and duties of his office.

AMENDMENT XXVI [1971]

SECTION 1. The right of citizens of the United States, who are eighteen years of age or older, to vote shall not be denied or abridged by the United States or by any State on account of age.

SECTION 2. The Congress shall have power to enforce this article by appropriate legislation.

NOTES

Chapter 1

1. *McCulloch v. Maryland*, 17 U.S. (4 Wheat.) 316, 407 (1819) (emphasis in original).

2. *Id.* at 403, 404 (quoting U.S. Const. preamble), 415 (emphasis in original), 407.

3. *Id.* at 407.

4. *Id.* at 404, 404, 405–406.

5. "All three branches of government...are agencies of the People. No branch, or combination of branches, can uniquely claim to speak for [the] People themselves; no branch is uniquely representative." Amar, Philadelphia Revisited: Amending the Constitution Outside Article V, 55 *U. Chi. L. Rev.* 1043, 1085 (1988). For opposing views, see J. Ely, *Democracy and Distrust* (1980); A. Bickel, *The Least Dangerous Branch* (1962).

"Human beings, if only to maintain a semblance of self-respect, have to be persuaded. Their consent must be sustained by opinions." E. Morgan, *Inventing the People* (1988), 1. "The great advantage of a constitutional convention, combined with popular ratification, was that it embodied the sovereignty of the whole people in the government and not simply in the locally elected representative branch. If a convention assigned adequate authority to the other branches and secured popular sanction for it, the local biases and shortsightedness of representatives would be checked by officers who were not tied to local constituents and who felt a larger responsibility to the whole." *Id.* at 261. "Although independence had determined that Americans were not part of the people of Great Britain, it had not determined whether they were one people or many, or whether the sovereignty of the people, say, of Virginia was exhausted in the creation of an independent government for Virginia. If Americans were in any sense one people, did that people enjoy a sovereignty too? And if so, who were their representatives?" *Id.* at 262.

6. Letter from Jefferson to William Charles Jarvis (Sept. 28, 1820), quoted in J. Bartlett, *Familiar Quotations* (15th ed. 1980), 389. Jefferson also wrote: "To consider the judges as the ultimate arbiters of all constitutional questions would place us under the despotism of an oligarchy." Quoted in A. Cox, *The Court and the Constitution* (1987), 123.

7. "In a government extending over the whole United States, tyrannies of the majority would be much less likely, because majorities would not be so easily put together. The multiplicity and diversity of interests in so large a territory would protect minorities, just as the multiplicity of religious sects in many states already prevented any one sect from gaining the majority needed to oppress the others." Morgan, *supra* note 5, at 269.

"The possibility [that a party to a contract might revoke it] proves the necessity of laying the foundations of our national government deeper than in the mere sanction of delegated authority. The fabric of American empire ought to rest on the solid basis of THE CONSENT OF THE PEOPLE. The streams of national power ought to flow immediately from that pure, original fountain of all legitimate authority." *The Federalist* No. 22, at 152 (A. Hamilton) (C. Rossiter ed. 1961).

8. In the opening paragraph of *McCulloch*, Justice Marshall

observed, "No tribunal can approach such a question without a deep sense of its importance, and of the awful responsibility involved in its decision. But it must be decided peacefully, or remain a source of hostile legislation, perhaps of hostility of a still more serious nature; and if it is to be so decided, by this tribunal alone can the decision be made." 17 U.S. (4 Wheat.) at 400–401.

The phrase "intelligent democracy" comes from Wedgwood, Freedom of Expression and Racial Speech, 8 *Tel Aviv U. Stud. L.* 325, 328 (1988): "The very meaning of intelligent democracy is the ability to contemplate all alternatives and to talk about them rationally."

9. On the supreme-law-of-the-land controversy, see Meese, The Law of the Constitution, 61 *Tul. L. Rev.* 979 (1987); *Marbury v. Madison*, 5 U.S. (1 Cranch) 137 (1803); U.S. Const. art. VI; *Cooper v. Aaron*, 358 U.S. 1 (1958).

10. Amar, *supra* note 5, at 1044.

11. U.S. Const. art. V provides: "The Congress, whenever two thirds of both Houses shall deem it necessary, shall propose Amendments to this Constitution, or, on the Application of the Legislatures of two thirds of the several States, shall call a Convention for proposing Amendments, which, in either Case, shall be valid to all Intents and Purposes, as Part of this Constitution, when ratified by the Legislatures of three fourths of the several States, or by Conventions in three fourths thereof, as the one or the other Mode of Ratification may be proposed by the Congress."

Professor Bruce Ackerman writes: "...Article V's affirmation of constitutional change through 'Convention' has not merely remained a textual possibility.... [T]he best interpretation of our constitutional history requires the legal conclusion that We the People of the United States have indeed amended our Constitution through 'Conventional' means." Ackerman, The Storrs Lectures: Discovering the Constitution, 93 *Yale L.J.* 1013, 1062 (1984). See generally *id.* at 1057–1070; Amar, Of Sovereignty and Federalism, 96 *Yale L.J.* 1425, 1464 (1987); Amar, Our Forgotten Constitution: A Bicentennial Comment, 97 *Yale L.J.* 281, 288–294 (1987).

For arguments against the amending of the Constitution by the Supreme Court through its decisions, see Justice Black's comments, *Bell v. Maryland, infra* note 41.

12. *The Federalist* No. 43, 278–279 (J. Madison) (C. Rossiter ed. 1961) observes: "That useful alterations [of the Constitution] will be suggested by experience could not but be foreseen. It was requisite, therefore, that a mode for introducing them should be provided. The mode preferred...guards equally against that extreme facility, which would render the Constitution too mutable; and that extreme difficulty, which might perpetuate its discovered faults. It, moreover, equally enables the general and the State governments to originate the amendment of errors, as they may be pointed out by experience."

Professor Charles L. Black Jr. writes: "If final power belongs to the people (and this is the democratic ideal toward which we aspire) then what is to prevent the ruthless trampling under, by most of the people, of the human rights of some of the people? The lines of an answer can be looked for only in the hope that the greater part of the people, having the power, will withhold themselves from exerting it in disregard of the rights of those who are powerless. It is very plain that the only control on final power must be self-control." C. Black, *The People and the Court* (1960), 106.

He adds: "On the theory that judicial review is a people's institution, confirmed by the people through history, the false antithesis between judicial action and the impulses of the people is dissolved. On this view, the people have projected on the Court a part of their desire—their long-range desire for tolerance and fairness, their desire, basic to all sanity, to restrain themselves by law. ...Living, vigorous judicial review (and this seems to me to be the deepest truth that can be stated about it) cannot be justified as something that thwarts and contradicts popular desire—but it can be justified as something that fulfills popular desire." *Id.* at 117.

13. *McCulloch*, 17 U.S. (4 Wheat.) at 407.

14. *Id.* at 414.

15. *Cf.* Nagel, The Formulaic Constitution, 84 *Mich. L. Rev.* 165 (1985).

16. *McCulloch*, 17 U.S. (4 Wheat.) at 415 (emphasis in original). See also Ackerman, Constitutional Politics/Constitutional Law, 99 *Yale L.J.* 453 (1989); Powell, Parchment Matters: A Meditation on the Constitution as Text, 71 *Iowa L. Rev.* 1427 (1986); Deutsch, Neutrality, Legitimacy, and the Supreme Court: Intersections between Law and Political Science, 20 *Stan. L. Rev.* 169 (1968).

17. 4 *The Records of the Federal Convention of 1787* (J. Hutson ed. 1987), 183. "Parts of the text in parentheses were 'crossed out of the original.'" *Id.* n.1 (quoting 4 *The Records of the Federal Convention of 1787* (M. Farrand ed. 1966), 37).

In a submission to the speaker of the Pennsylvania House of Representatives, dated Aug. 24, 1791, James Wilson, a member of the Constitutional Convention's Committee of Detail, wrote: "[H]ow can it become the foundation of practice, if the laws, and particularly the criminal laws, are written *in a manner* in which they cannot be clearly known or understood?...[An understandable] manner has been already adopted, with success, in the Constitution of the United States." 1 *The Works of James Wilson* (R. McCloskey ed. 1967), 63–64 (emphasis added).

18. *McCulloch*, 17 U.S. (4 Wheat.) at 415.

The attorney general of Maryland argued: "It is objected, that this act creates a corporation; which, being an exercise of a fundamental power of sovereignty, can only be claimed by Congress, under their grant of specific powers. But to have enumerated the power of establishing corporations among the specific powers of Congress, would have been to change the whole plan of the constitution; to destroy its simplicity, and load it with all the complex details of a code of private jurisprudence. The power of establishing a corporation is not one of the *ends* of government; it is only a class of *means* for accomplishing its ends. An enumeration of this particular class of means, omitting all others, would have been a useless anomaly in the constitution.... The United States are sovereign as to certain specific objects, and may, therefore, erect a corporation for the purpose of effecting those objects. If the incorporating power had been expressly granted as an *end*, it would have conferred a power not intended; if granted as a *means*, it would have conferred nothing more than was before given by necessary implication." *Id.* at 357–358 (emphasis in original).

19. The Court observed that the "instrument does not profess to enumerate the means by which the powers it confers may be executed; nor does it prohibit the creation of a corporation, if... essential to the beneficial exercise of those powers." *Id.* at 408–409. Among the enumerated powers of Article I, § 8 that might be facilitated, the Court noted "the great powers to lay and collect taxes; to borrow money; to regulate commerce; to declare and conduct a war; and to raise and support armies and navies." *Id.* at 407.

20. *Id.* at 421. Professor Nagel, with regard to this constitutional principle, writes: "Chief Justice Marshall's summarizing passage is an eerie precursor of the modern formulaic style. Today the passage would be written without the magisterial tone but otherwise would be little changed. It might look like this: Legislation under the necessary and proper clause is sufficiently justified if: (1) the purpose is legitimate and within the scope of the constitution; (2) the means chosen are appropriate or plainly adapted to that purpose; (3) the means are not specifically or impliedly prohibited." Nagel, *supra* note 15, at 187.

21. G. Gunther, *John Marshall's Defense of* McCulloch v. Maryland (1969), 5–6. For a powerful and fascinating examination of *McCulloch*, see J. White, *When Words Lose Their Meaning: Constitutions and Reconstitutions of Language, Character, and Community* (1984), 247–263, 354–361.

22. *McCulloch*, 17 U.S. (4 Wheat.) at 421.

23. *Id.* at 400.

24. *Id.*

25. *Id.* at 425.

26. *Id.* at 429 (emphasis added). A reader can almost hear Chief

Justice Marshall exclaim with relief, "We have a principle which is safe for the states and safe for the Union!"

"Madison recognized that [the convention] could achieve the objectives he had in mind for it only by appealing to a popular sovereignty not hitherto fully recognized, to the people of the United States as a whole. They alone could be thought to stand superior to the people of any single state.... [They would be] a people who constituted a separate and superior entity, capable of conveying to a national government an authority that would necessarily impinge on the authority of the state governments." Morgan, *supra* note 5, at 267.

27. *McCulloch*, 17 U.S. (4 Wheat.) at 431. The Court explained how this great constitutional principle specifically applied to a state's power to tax: "If we measure the power of taxation residing in a State, by the extent of sovereignty which the people of a single State possess, and can confer on its government, we have an intelligible standard, applicable to every case to which the power may be applied. We have a principle which leaves the power of taxing the people and property of a State unimpaired; which leaves to a State the command of all its resources, and which places beyond its reach, all those powers which are conferred by the people of the United States on the government of the Union, and all those means which are given for the purpose of carrying those powers into execution." *Id.* at 429–430.

28. *Id.* at 426.

29. *Id.* at 407.

30. *Webster v. Reproductive Health Services*, 492 U.S. 490 (1989).

31. *Roe v. Wade*, 410 U.S. 113, 164 (1972). Justice Stewart, concurring, said that the right to privacy "necessarily includes the right of a woman to decide whether or not to terminate her pregnancy." *Id.* at 170.

Prior to *Roe*, the Court had construed the Due Process Clause of the Fourteenth Amendment to include a right to privacy and recognized as one of its components "[t]he right of the individual, married or single, to be free from unwarranted governmental intrusion into matters so fundamentally affecting a person as the decision whether to bear or beget a child." *Eisenstadt v. Baird*, 405 U.S. 438, 453 (1972).

A possible factor contributing to the confusion between means and principle may be that the Court had come to perceive the right to privacy, prior to its decision in *Webster*, as being "vulnerable," as having something less than the status of a constitutional principle or provision. For a divided Court in *Bowers v. Hardwick*, 478 U.S. 186, 194 (1986), Justice White, in an opinion joined by Chief Justice Burger and Justices Powell, Rehnquist, and O'Connor, called the privacy right "judge-made constitutional law having little or no cognizable roots in the language or design of the Constitution."

32. *Webster*, 492 U.S. at 518.

33. *McCulloch*, 17 U.S. (4 Wheat.) at 421.

34. *Webster*, 492 U.S. at 548–549. Justice Blackmun also wrote: "The plurality does not even mention, much less join, the true jurisprudential debate underlying this case: whether the Constitution includes an 'unenumerated' general right to privacy. . . . [R]ather than arguing that the text of the Constitution makes no mention of the right to privacy, the plurality complains that the critical elements of the *Roe* framework—trimesters and viability—do not appear in the Constitution and are, therefore, somehow inconsistent with a Constitution cast in general terms. Were this a true concern, we would have to abandon most of our constitutional jurisprudence. As the plurality well knows, or should know, the 'critical elements' of countless constitutional doctrines nowhere appear in the Constitution's text. The Constitution makes no mention, for example, . . . of the rational-basis test, or the specific verbal formulations of intermediate and strict scrutiny by which this Court evaluates claims under the Equal Protection Clause. The reason is simple. Like the *Roe* framework, these tests or standards are not, and do not purport to be, rights protected by the Constitution. Rather, they are judge-made methods for evaluating and measuring the strength

and scope of constitutional rights or for balancing the constitutional rights of individuals against the competing interests of government." *Id.* at 546–548.

Chief Justice Rehnquist wrote in response: "JUSTICE BLACKMUN takes us to task for our failure to join in a 'great issues' debate as to whether the Constitution includes an 'unenumerated' general right to privacy as recognized in cases such as *Griswold v. Connecticut* and *Roe*. But *Griswold v. Connecticut*, unlike *Roe*, did not purport to adopt a whole framework, complete with detailed rules and distinctions, to govern the cases in which the asserted liberty interest would apply.... [The *Roe*] framework sought to deal with areas of medical practice traditionally subject to state regulations, and it sought to balance once and for all by reference only to the calendar the claims of the State to protect the fetus as a form of human life against the claims of a woman to decide for herself whether or not to abort a fetus she was carrying." *Id.* at 520 (citations omitted).

35. *McCulloch*, 17 U.S. (4 Wheat.) at 407. The risk of converting the Constitution from something sufficiently free of detail to be "embraced by the human mind" to something hardly understandable by the general public seems to be reflected in the exchange between Chief Justice Rehnquist and Justice Blackmun in note 34.

36. *Korematsu v. United States*, 323 U.S. 214, 225 (Frankfurter, J., concurring) (1944).

37. Henkin, *Shelley v. Kraemer:* Notes for a Revised Opinion, 110 *U. Pa. L. Rev.* 473, 505 (1962). For discussion of whether the Fourteenth Amendment protects groups, see Marshall, A Comment on the Nondiscrimination Principle in a "Nation of Minorities," 93 *Yale L.J.* 1006 (1984); Fiss, Groups and the Equal Protection Clause, 5 *Phil. & Pub. Aff.* 107 (1976).

38. "During the nineteenth century and down through the chief justiceship of Hughes, there were few separate, concurring, or dissenting opinions from the opinion for the Court's decision.... Individual opinions now predominate over institutional opinions for the Court.... When we compare the Burger Court's practice with

that of forty years ago, we find ten times the number of concurring opinions, four times more dissenting opinions, and seven times the number of separate opinions in which the justices explain their personal views and why they partially concur in and/or dissent from the Court's opinion.... Between 1901 and the last year of Chief Justice Warren, in 1969, there were 51 cases decided by plurality opinions. Between 1969 and 1984, however, the Burger Court handed down 111 plurality opinions, more plurality opinions than were rendered in the entire previous history of the Court." D. O'Brien, *Storm Center: The Supreme Court in American Politics* (1986), 262–264.

39. *Webster* (Syllabus), 492 U.S. at 498. See also *supra* note 34.

For an interesting examination of these developments, see Nagel, *supra* note 15, at 165: "[A] new style of opinion writing has emerged as the most common method of constitutional exegesis. This style emphasizes formalized doctrine expressed in elaborately layered sets of 'tests' or 'prongs' or 'requirements' or 'standards' or 'hurdles.' The judicial opinions in which these 'analytical devices' appear tend to be characterized by tireless, detailed debate among the Justices. The apparently definitive formulations, standing amidst a welter of separate opinions and contentious footnotes, seem forlorn testaments to the ideals of clarity and consensus. But, taken together, the formulae and the extensive explanation comprise a consistent pattern of earnest argumentation."

40. *Day-Brite Lighting v. Missouri*, 342 U.S. 421, 423 (1952).

41. *Ferguson v. Skrupa*, 372 U.S. 726, 730 (1963).

"[W]here the law is not prohibited,... to undertake here to determine the degree of its necessity, would be to pass the line which circumscribes the judicial department, and to tread on legislative ground. This court disclaims all pretensions to such a power." *McCulloch*, 17 U.S. (4 Wheat.) at 423.

"We admonished that in deciding this case we should remember that 'it is *a constitution* we are expounding.' We conclude as we do because we remember that it *is* a Constitution and that it is our duty 'to bow with respectful submission to its provisions.' And in recalling that it is a Constitution 'intended to endure for ages to come,' we also remember that the Founders wisely provided the means for that endurance: changes in the Constitution, when thought necessary, are to be proposed by Congress or conventions and ratified by the States. The Founders gave no such amending power to this Court. Our duty is simply to interpret the Constitution, and in doing so the test of constitutionality is not whether a law is offensive to our conscience or to the 'good old common law,' but whether it is offensive to the Constitution." *Bell v. Maryland*, 378 U.S. 226, 341–342 (1964) (Black, J., dissenting) (footnotes and citations omitted) (emphasis in original).

42. This book is not concerned with whether Justice Marshall was correct when he wrote, "Courts are the mere instruments of the law. . . . Judicial power is never exercised for the purpose of giving effect to the will of the Judge; always for the purpose of giving effect . . . to the will of the law." *Osborn v. U.S. Bank*, 22 U.S. (9 Wheat.) 738, 866 (1824). Nor is it concerned with whether the French jurist Saleilles had it right when he wrote, "One wills at the beginning the result; one finds the principle afterwards; such is the genesis of all juridical construction." Saleilles, *De la personnalité juridique*, translated and quoted in B. Cardozo, *The Nature of the Judicial Process* (1921), 170.

After juxtaposing Saleilles's words with Marshall's, Cardozo wrote, "So sweeping a statement exaggerates the element of free volition. It ignores the factors of determinism which cabin and confine within narrow bounds the range of unfettered choice. None the less, by its very excess of emphasis, it supplies the needed corrective of an ideal of impossible objectivity." *Id.*

43. Dworkin, Hard Cases, 88 *Harv. L. Rev.* 1057, 1060 (1975).

44. Cardozo, *supra* note 42, at 7.

45. "In expounding the Constitution, the Court's role is to discern 'principles sufficiently absolute to give them roots throughout the community and continuity over significant periods of time, and to lift them above the level of the pragmatic political judgments

of a particular time and place.' " *University of California Regents v. Bakke*, 438 U.S. 265, 299 (1978) (quoting A. Cox, *The Role of the Supreme Court in American Government* (1976), 114).

46. See Ackerman, *supra* note 16; Powell, *supra* note 16.

Chapter 2

1. *National League of Cities v. Usery*, 426 U.S. 833 (1976).

2. U.S. Const. amend. X provides: "The powers not delegated to the United States by the Constitution, nor prohibited by it to the States, are reserved to the States." U.S. Const. art. I, § 8, cl. 3 empowers Congress "to regulate Commerce . . . among the several States."

3. *Maryland v. Wirtz*, 392 U.S. 183 (1968).

4. *National League*, 426 U.S. at 845. Wage and hour regulations are based on the Fair Labor Standards Act of 1938, 52 Stat. 1060, 29 U.S.C. § 201 *et seq.* (1940 ed.). The act initially excluded the states from its coverage. In 1974 the exclusion was removed by 88 Stat. 55, 29 U.S.C. § 203(d), § 203(s)(5), and § 203(x) (1970 Ed., Supp. IV).

5. *National League*, 426 U.S. at 851.

6. *Id.* at 852 (emphasis added).

7. *Id.* at 856 (Blackmun, J., concurring) (reference omitted) (emphasis added).

8. *Id.* at 880 (Stevens, J., dissenting).

9. *Id.* at 881.

10. *Id.* at 871–872 (Brennan, J., dissenting).

11. *Id.* at 856 (Blackmun, J., concurring).

12. *Id.*

13. *Id.*

14. *Id.*

15. Hart, The Supreme Court, 1958 Term—Foreword: The Time Chart of the Justices, 73 *Harv. L. Rev.* 84, 111 (1959).

16. *National League*, 426 U.S. at 852.

17. The decision was announced on the last day of the term. Under the Court's rules, postponement would have required scheduling reargument of the case in the next term. The rule, designed to keep the work of the Court current, sometimes results in what has come to be called a June opinion—"an opinion on which time ran out, leaving the ragged edges glaringly apparent." See Greenhouse, Washington Talk–Justice, *N.Y. Times*, May 26, 1989, at A12, col. 1.

18. *National League*, 426 U.S. at 853 (quoting *Fry v. United States*, 421 U.S. 542, 548 (1975)).

19. *National League*, 426 U.S. at 840, 854.

20. *Fry*, 421 U.S. at 549.

21. See *Garcia v. San Antonio Metro Transit Authority*, 469 U.S. 528, 540 (1985).

22. *National League*, 426 U.S. at 881 (Stevens, J., dissenting). When and whether justices should express their personal view of legislation in an opinion raises questions that deserve attention but that I do not address in this book.

23. *Sherman v. United States*, 356 U.S. 369 (1958).

24. *National League*, 426 U.S. at 852.

25. *Garcia*, 469 U.S. at 579–580 (Rehnquist, J., dissenting): "JUSTICE POWELL's reference to the 'balancing test' approved in *National League of Cities* is not identical with the language in that case, which recognized that Congress could not act under its commerce power to infringe on certain fundamental aspects of state sovereignty that are essential to 'the States' separate and independent existence.' Nor is either test, or JUSTICE O'CONNOR's suggested approach, precisely congruent with JUSTICE BLACKMUN's views in 1976."

Not only is there confusion about whether balancing is a part of the *National League of Cities* test, there is also confusion among the justices who believe the test incorporates balancing. There is no shared understanding about its meaning.

26. *Garcia*, 469 U.S. at 581 (O'Connor, J., dissenting).

27. Kaufman, Judges or Scholars: To Whom Shall We Look for Our Constitutional Values, 37 *J. Legal Educ.* 184, 190 (1987).

28. C. Black, *Perspectives in Constitutional Law* (1963), 30, quoted in *Garcia*, 469 U.S. at 581 (O'Connor, J., dissenting).

29. Reed, *Stare Decisis* and Constitutional Law, 9 *Pa. B.A. Q.* 131 (1938).

30. *Garcia*, 469 U.S. at 557.

31. *Id.* at 559 (Powell, J., dissenting) (quoting *Arizona v. Rumsey*, 467 U.S. 203, 212 (1984)).

32. *Garcia*, 469 U.S. at 546–547. Rejected, too, was the Court's reformulation of the rule in *Hodel v. Virginia Surface Mining & Recl. Assn.*, 452 U.S. 264 (1981). There the Court followed, to use Professor Nagel's term, the "formulaic style." The Court stated that "four conditions must be satisfied before a state activity may be deemed immune from a particular federal regulation under the Commerce Clause. First, . . . the federal statute at issue must regulate 'the "States as States." ' Second, the statute must 'address matters that are indisputably "attribute[s] of state sovereignty." ' Third, state compliance with the federal obligation must 'directly impair [the States'] ability "to structure integral operations in areas of traditional governmental functions." ' Finally, the relation of state and federal interests must not be such that 'the nature of the federal interest . . . justifies state submission.' " *Garcia*, 469 U.S. at 537 (quoting *Hodel*, 452 U.S. at 287–288, and n.29 (quoting *National League*, 426 U.S., at 845, 852, 854)). See Nagel, The Formulaic Constitution, 84 *Mich. L. Rev.* 165, 187–189 (1985).

33. *Garcia*, 469 U.S. at 536 (quoting *Garcia v. San Antonio Metro Transit Authority*, 557 F. Supp. 445, 453 (1983)).

34. *Garcia*, 469 U.S. at 546–547.

35. *Id.* at 558, 559 (Powell, J., dissenting).

36. *Id.* at 559.

37. *Id.* at 580 (Rehnquist, J., dissenting).

Should it not be incumbent on justices to spell out, if they can, the details of the constitutional principle on which their dissents rest? If they cannot, should they not acknowledge this, as does Justice Rehnquist in *Hustler Magazine v. Falwell*, 485 U.S. 46 (1988)? There he searched for and failed to discover a principled standard for drawing a line between protected and unprotected speech under the First Amendment. For the Court, he observed with candor: "If it were possible by laying down a principled standard to separate [the "outrageous" from more traditional cartoons] public discourse would probably suffer little or no harm. But we doubt that there is any such standard, and we are quite sure that the pejorative description 'outrageous' does not supply one." *Id.* at 55.

Similarly, Justice Brennan for the Court in *Garcia* said "that the attempt to draw boundaries of state regulatory immunity in terms of 'traditional governmental function' is not only unworkable but is also inconsistent with established principles of federalism." *Garcia*, 469 U.S. at 531.

38. *Id.* at 589 (O'Connor, J., dissenting).

39. *Mitchell v. W. T. Grant Co.*, 416 U.S. 600, 627–628 (1973) (Powell, J., concurring).

40. W. Douglas, Stare Decisis: *Eighth Annual Benjamin N. Cardozo Lecture to the Association of the Bar of the City of New York* (1949), 24.

Chapter 3

1. *Cooper v. Aaron*, 358 U.S. 1 (1958).

2. *Id.* at 5.

3. *Aaron v. Cooper*, 257 F.2d 33, 34 (8th Cir. 1958).

4. *Id.*

5. *Id.* at 37.

6. *Id.* at 40.

7. *Id.* (emphasis in original).

8. Farber, The Supreme Court and the Rule of Law: *Cooper v. Aaron* Revisited, 1982 *U. Ill. L. Rev.* 387.

9. *Cooper*, 358 U.S. at 4.

10. *Id.*

"The Court wanted the world to know that it was speaking with absolutely a single voice. Thus *Cooper v. Aaron*, a stern rebuke to segregationist states, was signed by each of the justices." R. Posner, *The Federal Courts: Crisis and Reform* (1985), 127. See also Gewirtz, Remedies and Resistance, 92 *Yale L.J.* 585, 626–628 (1983); Hutchinson, Unanimity and Desegregation: Decisionmaking in the Supreme Court, 1948–1958, 68 *Geo. L.J.* 1 (1979).

11. *Cooper*, 358 U.S. at 7.

12. *Aaron*, 257 F.2d at 35.

13. *Cooper*, 358 U.S. at 7.

14. *Id.* at 18. The supreme-law-of-the-land pronouncement, the focus of much critical comment, is not examined here. For citations, see Farber, *supra* note 8, at 387–390; Meese, The Law of the Constitution, 61 *Tul. L. Rev.* 979 (1987).

15. *Cooper*, 358 U.S. at 16–17 (citation omitted).

16. Chief Justice Gardner, dissenting in *Aaron v. Cooper*, said, "The action of Judge Lemley [to suspend the plan of integration] was based on realities and on conditions, rather than theories." *Aaron*, 257 F.2d at 41.

17. *Cooper*, 358 U.S. at 19–20.

18. All Things Considered (National Public Radio broadcast, Jan. 30, 1987).

19. *Briggs v. Elliott*, 132 F. Supp. 776, 777 (E.D.S.C. 1955) (emphasis added). See D. Garrow, *Bearing the Cross* (1986), 83, for a description of a mass meeting in December 1957, six or seven months before *Cooper*, at which Martin Luther King, Jr., announced for the first time that the Montgomery Improvement Society was looking beyond integrating the bus system. "We must have integrated schools. . . . That is when our race will gain full equality. We cannot rest . . . until every public school is integrated."

20. R. Kluger, *Simple Justice* (1975), 752.

21. *Aaron*, 257 F.2d at 39.

22. For an opposing view, see Rostow, American Legal Realism and the Sense of the Profession, 34 *Rocky Mtn. L. Rev.* 123, 142 (1962): "Exercising high political powers, the Court must have a high sense of strategy and tactics. Its influence on our public life

depends in large part on the Court's skill in advocacy, and its sensitivity to the powerful forces which from time to time, in different combinations, must resist its will."

23. *Aaron v. McKinley*, 173 F. Supp. 944, 947 (E.D. Ark. 1968). The court permanently enjoined the defendants and their successors in office "from engaging in any acts which will ... impede, thwart, delay or frustrate the execution of the approved plan for the gradual integration of the schools." *Id*. at 952.

24. The vote at the election was about 19,000 against and 7,500 for the plan. *Id*. at 947.

25. *Cooper*, 358 U.S. at 7.

26. On candor, see Shapiro, In Defense of Judicial Candor, 100 *Harv. L. Rev.* 731 (1987); G. Calabresi, *A Common Law for the Age of Statutes* (1982), 176–181. On descriptive scrupulousness—the search for the exact word and phrase—as one of the craft values of well-written opinions, see Posner, Law and Literature: A Relation Reargued, 72 *Va. L. Rev.* 1351, 1390 (1986). See also Rostow, *supra* note 22.

Chapter 4

1. *Brown v. Board of Education*, 347 U.S. 483 (1954) [hereinafter *Brown I*]; 349 U.S. 294 (1955) [hereinafter *Brown II*].

2. *Plessy v. Ferguson*, 163 U.S. 537 (1896).

3. *Brown I*, 347 U.S. at 495.

4. *Id*. The Fourteenth Amendment, ratified on July 9, 1868, provides in pertinent part: "No state shall ... deny to any person within its jurisdiction the equal protection of the laws."

5. *Bolling v. Sharpe*, 347 U.S. 497, 500 (1954). The Fifth Amendment, ratified on Dec. 15, 1791, provides in pertinent part: "No person shall ... be deprived of life, liberty, or property, without due process of law."

6. D. O'Brien, *Storm Center: The Supreme Court in American Politics* (1986), 281.

7. *Brown I*, 347 U.S. at 486 n.1.

8. R. Kluger, *Simple Justice* (1975), 521.

9. *Id.*

10. "Behind many of the most important decisions we make ...are judgments of principle that do not reduce to balancing.... The same is true for some of our most important constitutional decisions. It is difficult to read *Brown v. Board of Education* as based on a conscious, or unconscious, balancing of the interests. ...[T]he Court based its decision...on the intolerability of racial discrimination." Aleinikoff, Constitutional Law in the Age of Balancing, 96 *Yale L.J.* 943, 998 (1987).

Aleinikoff's conclusion can be reached only by ignoring *Brown II*, where the Court said that it may, in accord with unidentified equity principles, authorize the denial of constitutional rights to persons whose rights it has already declared to have been violated.

Aleinikoff responds to this critique by suggesting that "*Brown II* is really a remedies case, which invokes traditional equitable (read: law-making) powers of the courts; thus it is more appropriate to balance there" than in a "rights" case. Letter from Alexander Aleinikoff to Joseph Goldstein (Oct. 11, 1988).

11. *Brown I*, 347 U.S. at 495–496; *Bolling*, 347 U.S. at 500.

12. *Brown I*, 347 U.S. at 495.

13. *Id.* at 495 n.13.

14. *Id.* at 495.

15. *Id.* at 496.

16. *Id.* at 495.

17. *Bolling*, 347 U.S. at 500.

18. *Brown I*, 347 U.S. at 492, cites both *Sweatt v. Painter*, 339 U.S. 629 (1950), and *McLaurin v. Oklahoma State Regents*, 339 U.S. 637 (1950).

19. *Sweatt*, 339 U.S. at 635.

20. *Bolling*, 347 U.S. at 499–500 (citing *Korematsu v. United States*, 323 U.S. 214, 216 (1944)).

21. *Brown I*, 347 U.S. at 495. Similar reasoning is used in *Bolling*, 347 U.S. at 500. See Elman, The Solicitor General's Office,

Justice Frankfurter, and Civil Rights Litigation, 1946–1960: An Oral History, 100 *Harv. L. Rev.* 817, 827–830 (1987).

The Court also called for reargument because the cases were class actions. But "[p]rimarily because of the opposition of Justices Black and Douglas [to relief being granted to "those similarly situated in their respective school districts"], the final *Brown II* opinion restricted relief 'to the parties to these cases only.' " B. Schwartz, *Swann's Way* (1986), 48. This issue is also discussed in Kluger, *supra* note 8, at 686.

22. *Brown II*, 349 U.S. at 298.

23. *Id.* at 301.

24. *Id.* at 298 n.2 (quoting *Brown I*, 347 U.S. at 495 n.13).

25. *Brown II*, 349 U.S. at 299.

26. *Id.*

27. *Id.*

28. *Id.* at 298 n.2 (quoting *Brown I*, 347 U.S. at 496 n.13).

29. *Brown II*, 349 U.S. at 300.

30. *Id.* at 298 n.2 (emphasis added) (quoting *Brown I*, 347 U.S. at 496 n.13).

31. *Brown II*, 349 U.S. at 301.

32. H. McClintock, *Handbook of the Principles of Equity* (2d ed. 1948), 70–71.

33. *Id.* at 52.

Justice Frankfurter, concurring in *Youngstown v. Sawyer*, 343 U.S. 579, 609–610 (1952), said, " 'Balancing the equities' when considering whether an injunction should issue is lawyers' jargon for choosing between conflicting public interests. When Congress itself has struck the balance, has defined the weight to be given the competing interests, a court of equity is not justified in ignoring that pronouncement under the guise of exercising equitable discretion."

34. McClintock, *supra* note 32, at 52.

35. *Brown I*, 347 U.S. at 495.

36. *Korematsu*, 323 U.S. at 216.

37. Justice Frankfurter circulated a memorandum to the Court on January 15, 1954. In it he stated:

"1. A decree in this case in favor of the appellants of necessity would be drastically different from decrees enforcing merely individual rights before the Court.... Even in the cases involving higher education the Court was dealing with individuals, not merely the one or few before the Court, but all who would be affected by the results of the individual litigations were few in number. Thus, the problem presented was amenable to individual treatment. This is not so in the situations before us.

"2. To be sure, we have formally before us only individual claimants.... This fact, however, does not change the essential subject matter of the litigation—we are asked in effect to transform state-wide school systems. Declaration of unconstitutionality is not a wand by which such transformations can be accomplished. Assuming the best will in the world the transformation sought involves physical and education changes which in turn depend on considerations affecting the utilization or improvisation of buildings, educational administration (what teachers, for whom, under what circumstances) budgetary matters, and the factor of time in bringing about the required result.

"3. ... The heart of the matter is the meaning of 'integrated'— what is implied by it. Integration, that is 'equal protection,' can readily be achieved by lowering the standards certainly of those who at the start are, in the phrase of George Orwell, 'more equal.' But 'integration' could lower the standards of those now under discrimination. It would indeed make a mockery of the Constitutional process in vindicating a claim to equal treatment to achieve 'integrated' but lower education standards. I assume that it is a fair assumption that in enforcing the Fourteenth Amendment the Court is, broadly speaking, promoting a process of social betterment and not of social deterioration. A Court being fallible and finite cannot in a day change a deplorable situation into the ideal. It does its duty if it gets effectively under way the righting of a wrong, and when the wrong is a rooted historic process does its duty if it effectuates steps that reverse the direction of the wrong process."

Memorandum from Justice Frankfurter to the Court (Jan. 15, 1954) (Frankfurter Papers, Harvard University). See Kluger, *supra* note 8, at 685 *et seq.*, concerning the circulation of this memorandum.

These issues were resolved by the Court by implication.

38. Fourteen years after *Brown II*, the Court in a *per curiam* opinion declared, without explaining why, that delay in "desegregation is no longer constitutionally permissible." *Alexander v. Holmes County Board of Education*, 396 U.S. 19, 20 (1969).

39. *Brown II*, 349 U.S. at 300 (emphasis added) (footnote omitted).

40. *Alexander v. Hillman*, 296 U.S. 222, 239 (1935), cited in *Brown II*, 349 U.S. at 300.

41. *Brown II*, 349 U.S. at 300.

42. *Alexander*, 296 U.S. at 240.

43. *Hecht Co. v. Bowles*, 321 U.S. 321, 329–330 (1944).

44. *Brown II*, 349 U.S. at 300.

45. *Hecht*, 321 U.S. at 330.

46. *Id.* at 329–330.

47. *Brown II*, 349 U.S. at 300 (emphasis added) (footnotes omitted).

48. *Id.* at 300–301.

49. *Id.* at 300.

50. *Sweatt*, 339 U.S. at 635 (quoting *Sipuel v. Board of Regents*, 332 U.S. 631, 633 (1948)).

51. "Robert Carter, arguing the Topeka case, and Louis Redding, handling Delaware, both asked for 'forthwith' decrees from the Court—that is, an order for immediate desegregation—and James Nabrit, winding up his five-year involvement with the District of Columbia case, offered the Court a sample of the wording he proposed for a decree ending Washington school segregation just as promptly, and without any 'option plan' favoring white students. Now was the moment for a firm decision by the Court, said Nabrit." Kluger, *supra* note 8, at 736.

To North Carolina's strong plea for mark-time desegregation

to save its celebrated school system, Thurgood Marshall said that the argument to postpone enforcement of a constitutional right "is never made until Negroes are involved. And then for some reason this [Negro] population of our country is constantly asked, 'Well, for the sake of the group that has denied you these rights all of this time,' as the attorney general of North Carolina said, 'to protect their greatest and most cherished heritage, that the Negroes should give up their rights.' If by any stretch of the imagination any other minority group had been involved in this case, we would never have been here." *Id.* at 736.

52. *Korematsu*, 323 U.S. at 216 (emphasis added).

53. *Bolling*, 347 U.S. at 499.

54. Black, The Unfinished Business of the Warren Court, 46 *Wash. L. Rev.* 3, 22 (1970). The notion that the Constitution, which limits what government can do, exempts the judicial branch of government, particularly the Supreme Court, from its restraints is beyond understanding. "[T]he particular phraseology of the constitution of the United States confirms and strengthens the principle, supposed to be essential to all written constitutions, . . . that *courts,* as well as other departments, are bound by that instrument." *Marbury v. Madison,* 5 U.S. (1 Cranch) 137, 180 (1803) (emphasis in original).

55. Posner, Law and Literature: A Relation Reargued, 72 *Va. L. Rev.* 1351, 1390 (1986).

56. *Brown II*, 349 U.S. at 301.

57. *New York Times Co. v. United States*, 403 U.S. 713 (1971).

58. Justice Black wrote concerning the First Amendment: "I believe that every moment's continuance of the injunctions against these newspapers amounts to a flagrant, indefensible, and continuing violation of the First Amendment. . . . In my view it is unfortunate that some of my Brethren are apparently willing to hold that the publication of news may sometimes be enjoined." *Id.* at 714–715.

59. Justice Black in conference is reported to have said: "Noth-

ing [is] more important than that this Court should not issue what it cannot enforce." Kluger, *supra* note 8, at 740.

60. "The judiciary ... has no influence over either the sword or the purse; no direction either of the strength or of the wealth of the society, and can take no active resolution whatever. It may truly be said to have neither FORCE nor WILL but merely judgment." *The Federalist* No. 78, at 465 (A. Hamilton) (C. Rossiter ed. 1961) (emphasis in original).

61. *Brown II*, 349 U.S. at 300. The Leveller John Warr noted in a 1649 pamphlet: "Why, under pretence of equity, and a court of conscience, are our wrongs doubled and trebled upon us, the court chancery being as extortionous, or more than any other court?" J. Warr, *The Corruption and Deficiency of the Laws of England* (London 1649), reprinted in 3 *Harleian Miscellany* (London 1744–1746), 250, 257.

62. Berlin, Equality, 56 *Proceedings of the Aristotelian Society* 301, 324 (1955–1956).

63. *Marbury*, 5 U.S. (1 Cranch) at 163.

64. *Brown II*, 349 U.S. at 301.

65. *Id.* (emphasis added).

66. *Brown I*, 347 U.S. at 487 n.1.

67. *Brown II*, 349 U.S. at 301.

68. Following *Brown I* and prior to *Brown II*, the School Board of Little Rock, "recognizing its responsibility to comply with Federal Constitutional requirements, ... approved a 'Plan of School Integration,' ... beginning with the high school level, in the fall of 1957." *Aaron v. Cooper*, 257 F.2d 33, 35 (8th Cir. 1958). For more on *Aaron v. Cooper*, see Chapter 3.

Chapter 5

1. *Regents of the University of California v. Bakke*, 438 U.S. 265, 274 (1978) (Powell, J.).

2. 42 U.S.C. § 2000d (1989).

3. *Bakke*, 438 U.S. at 271 n.† (Powell, J.).

4. *Id.* at 325 (Brennan, White, Marshall, and Blackmun, JJ., concurring in the judgment in part and dissenting in part).

5. *Id.* at 287 (Powell, J.).

6. *Id.* at 296 n.36.

7. *Id.* at 287, 320.
"The denial to [Bakke] of this right to individualized consideration without regard to his race is the principal evil of [the medical school] special admissions program." *Id.* at 318 n.52.

8. *Id.* at 271.

9. *Id.* at 272.

10. *Id.* at 271–272.

11. *Id.* at 325 (Brennan, White, Marshall, and Blackmun, JJ., concurring in the judgment in part and dissenting in part).

12. *Id.*

13. *Id.* at 408 n.1 (Stevens, J., concurring in the judgment in part and dissenting in part).

14. *Id.*

15. *Id.* at 287 (Powell, J.); *id.* at 325 (Brennan, White, Marshall, and Blackmun, JJ., concurring in the judgment in part and dissenting in part).

16. *Id.* at 281–320 (Powell, J.); *id.* at 421 (Stevens, J., concurring in the judgment in part and dissenting in part).

17. *Id.* at 289–290 (Powell, J.).

18. *Id.* at 325 (Brennan, White, Marshall, and Blackmun, JJ., concurring in the judgment in part and dissenting in part).

19. *Id.* at 294–295 n.34 (Powell, J.).

20. *Id.* at 320. *Id.* at 328 (Brennan, White, Marshall, and Blackmun, JJ., concurring in the judgment in part and dissenting in part).

21. *Id.* at 306 (Powell, J.).

22. *Id.* at 311.

23. *Id.* at 315.

24. *Id.*

25. *Id.* at 296 n.36.

26. See Monaghan, *Stare Decisis* and Constitutional Adjudication, 88 *Colum. L. Rev.* 723 (1988); Monaghan, Taking Supreme Court Opinions Seriously, 39 *Md. L. Rev.* 1 (1979).

Relatively few lower courts have cited Brennan's "central meaning" statement as precedent. However, it appears that at least two district courts have relied on the statement as authority. One wrote that in *Bakke*, "*five* members of the Court held that government may take race into account 'to remedy disadvantages cast on minorities by past racial prejudice, at least when appropriate findings have been made by judicial, legislative or administrative bodies with competence to act in this area.'" *Pettinaro Construction Co. v. Delaware Authority for Regional Transit*, 500 F. Supp. 559, 564 (Del. 1980) (emphasis added). Another wrote that the "opinion of Justices Brennan, White, Marshall and Blackmun summarized the meaning of the Court's opinion in *Bakke*" with the "central meaning" statement, and notes that "Justice Stevens criticizes... but Justice Powell does not disavow this statement." *Baker v. City of Detroit*, 483 F. Supp. 930, 989 (E.D. Mich. 1979). Similarly, still another court wrote that "the Supreme Court has held that quota-type affirmative action is unconstitutional where not supported by 'appropriate findings... made by judicial, legislative or administrative bodies with competence to act.'" *Associated General Contractors of California v. San Francisco Unified School District*, 616 F.2d 1381, 1390 n.14 (9th Cir. 1980).

Other courts, however, have interpreted the "central meaning" statement as a mischaracterization of the Court's judgment or as a summary of the Brennan four opinion. See, e.g., *Fullilove v. Kreps*, 584 F.2d 600, 603 n.3 (2d Cir. 1978); *Morrow v. Dillard*, 580 F.2d 1284, 1293 n.10 (5th Cir. 1978).

27. Justice Jackson, concurring in *Schwegmann Brothers v. Calvert Distillers Corp.*, 341 U.S. 384, 395–397 (1951), observed, "Resort to legislative history is only justified where the face of the Act is inescapably ambiguous.... Laws are intended for all of our people to live by; and people go to law offices to learn what their rights under those laws are.... To accept legislative debates to mod-

ify statutory provisions is to make the law inaccessible to a large part of the country." The same may be said even more strongly of using behind-the-scenes communications to interpret a decision that the Court has reached.

28. B. Schwartz, *Behind Bakke: Affirmative Action and the Supreme Court* (1988), 138–139.

29. *Id.* at 139.

30. *Id.*

31. *Id.* (emphasis added).

32. *Bakke*, 438 U.S. at 325 (Brennan, White, Marshall, and Blackmun, JJ., concurring in the judgment in part and dissenting in part) (emphasis added).

33. Schwartz, *supra* note 28, at 140 (emphasis in original).

34. *Id.*

35. *Id.* (emphasis added).

36. *Id.*

37. *Id.* at 141.

38. *Id.* at 150 n.3.

39. L. Powell, Proposed Statement from the Bench (June 26, 1978) (Manuscript Division, Library of Congress). Professor Schwartz provided the author with a copy of the full statement, which is summarized in detail at 143–146 of his book.

40. Schwartz, *supra* note 28, at 148.

41. For a sample of the varied readings of *Bakke*, see the following articles in *Regulation* (Sept./Oct. 1978): Sindler, The Court's Three Decisions; Jackson, Reparations Are Justified for Blacks; Sowell, Landmark or Curiosity?; Novak, Questions for the Court; Bork, A Murky Future; Marshall, Conversation with a Dean of Admissions. See also Abernathy, Affirmative Action and the Rule of *Bakke*, 64 *A.B.A. J.* 1233 (1978); Bell, Karst, Horowitz, Jones, White, Sedler, Gertner, Larson, Ginger, Motley, *Bakke* Symposium: Civil Rights Perspectives, 14 *Harv. C.R.-C.L. L. Rev.* (1979); Douglas, Bell, Blasi, Dixon, Greenawalt, Henkin, O'Neil, Posner, Symposium: *Regents of the University of California v. Bakke*, 67 *Calif. L. Rev.* 1 (1979); Lesnick, What Does *Bakke* Require of Law

Schools?, 128 *U. Pa. L. Rev.* 141 (1979); Maltz, A *Bakke* Primer, 32 *Okla. L. Rev.* 119 (1979).

42. This warning note is not reproduced with the syllabus to opinions in *U.S. Reports*, though it does appear in West Publishing Company's *Supreme Court Reporter*.

43. *United States v. Detroit Lumber Co.*, 200 U.S. 321, 337 (1906).

Chapter 6

1. 5 *Encyclopedia Britannica* (1971), 251.

2. Yo-Yo Ma: A Month at Tanglewood (Arts & Entertainment Network broadcast, May 10, 1990).

3. Quoted in Murphy, Marshaling the Court: Leadership, Bargaining, and the Judicial Process, 29 *U. Chi. L. Rev.* 640, 667 (1962).

4. R. Jackson, *The Supreme Court in the American System of Government* (1955), 16.

5. Brennan, State Court Decisions and the Supreme Court, 34 *Fla. B. J.* 269, 273 (1960).

Chief Justice Melville Weston Fuller, who served on the Court from 1888 to 1910, is said to have "deliberately cultivated personal friendships with every single Justice, whatever the man's views or propensities. He presided over the Justices' private conferences with unusual grace and saving wit. It was Fuller who originated the now-famous practice of each Justice shaking hands with every other Justice as they begin their conferences, and before they enter the courtroom." R. Shnayerson, *The Illustrated History of the Supreme Court of the United States* (1986), 150.

6. Quoted by Johnnetta B. Cole, president of Spelman College, speaking on behalf of herself and others receiving honorary degrees from New York University, May 17, 1990.

7. These canons have been influenced by my reading of J. White, *When Words Lose Their Meaning: Constitutions and Reconstitu-*

tions of Language, Character, and Community (1984); White, The Judicial Opinion and the Poem: Ways of Reading, Ways of Life, 82 *Mich. L. Rev.* 1669 (1984); F. Coffin, *The Ways of a Judge: Reflections from the Federal Appellate Bench* (1980); and Posner, Law and Literature: A Relation Reargued, 72 *Va. L. Rev.* 1351, 1386 (1986), who notes: "We need canons of judicial style."

8. The form of these canons and some of the words are from Edmund Randolph's "Draft Sketch of the Constitution," which the Constitutional Convention's Committee of Detail used as a working document. 4 *The Records of the Federal Convention of 1787* (J. Hutson ed. 1987), 183.

The quotation is from an Aug. 24, 1791, letter to the speaker of the Pennsylvania House of Representatives by James Wilson, a delegate to the Constitutional Convention. 1 *The Works of James Wilson* (R. McCloskey ed. 1967), 62 (emphasis in original).

9. Conversation with Professor Walter Dellinger, clerk to Justice Black in 1968–1969 (May 18, 1990). See also J. Frank, *Mr. Justice Black: The Man and His Opinions* (1949), 136: "[T]he Justice and his clerk may go over the opinion together, aloud, word for word. The objects will be threefold: first, to make the opinion as short as possible; second, to make it as clear as possible; and third, to put it in as simple language as possible."

10. Rostow, The Democratic Character of Judicial Review, 66 *Harv. L. Rev.* 193, 208 (1952).

11. Graubard, Doing Badly and Feeling Confused, *Daedalus*, Spring 1990, at 257.

12. Botstein, Damaged Literacy: Illiteracies and American Democracy, *Daedalus*, Spring 1990, at 61.

13. *Id.* at 77.

14. W. Douglas, Stare Decisis: *Eighth Annual Benjamin N. Cardozo Lecture to the Association of the Bar of the City of New York* (1949), 31.

15. J. Vining, *The Authoritative and the Authoritarian* (1986), 30.

16. J. Wilkinson, *Serving Justice: A Supreme Court Clerk's View* (1974), 92.

17. Vining, *supra* note 15, at 43 (emphasis in original).

18. *McCulloch v. Maryland*, 17 U.S. (4 Wheat.) 316, 414 (1819).

19. Arnold, Professor Hart's Theology, 73 *Harv. L. Rev.* 1298, 1312 (1960).

20. *Educational Films Corp. v. Ward*, 282 U.S. 379 (1931).

21. Powell, An Imaginary Judicial Opinion, 44 *Harv. L. Rev.* 889 (1931).

22. Quoted in Murphy, *supra* note 3, at 667.

23. Rostow, American Legal Realism and the Sense of the Profession, 34 *Rocky Mtn. L. Rev.* 123, 142 (1962).

24. W. Rehnquist, *The Supreme Court: How It Was, How It Is* (1987), 302.

25. Jackson, *supra* note 4, at 18–19.

26. Coffin, *supra* note 7, at 181.

27. Rehnquist, The Supreme Court: Past and Present, 59 *A.B.A. J.* 361, 363 (1973).

28. Tribe, On Reading the Constitution, 1988 *Utah L. Rev.* 747, 798.

29. Mikva, Goodbye to Footnotes, 56 *U. Colo. L. Rev.* 647, 648 (1985).

30. *Nixon v. Fitzgerald*, 457 U.S. 731 (1982).

31. Balkin, The Footnote, 83 *Nw. U.L. Rev.* 275, 280 (1989).

32. *Nixon*, 457 U.S. at 749.

33. *Id.*

34. *Id.* at 749 n.27.

35. *Id.* at 758 (Burger, C.J., concurring).

36. *Id.* at 763.

37. *Id.* at 763–764 n.7 (citations omitted).

38. *Id.* at 792 n.37 (White, J., dissenting).

39. *Id.* at 793 n.37.

40. *Id.* at 792.

41. Mikva, *supra* note 29, at 651.

42. Rehnquist, *supra* note 24, at 288–289.

43. "Within a single generation the justices have quadrupled the number of their law clerks.... The short stint by the bright, young, just-graduated law student, who moved into an intimate relationship with an old justice, kept him fresh, and then moved quickly on into a separate life and career, has already begun to be replaced by a job description and a job....

"[C]lerks routinely now say in private that they wrote one or another important opinion and that it was published with hardly a change.... However veiled the actual operations of the Supreme Court may be, we know that a large professional staff must have something to do. All are working to produce a product." Vining, *supra* note 15, at 10–11.

44. Hart, The Supreme Court 1958 Term—Foreword: The Time Chart of the Justices, 73 *Harv. L. Rev.* 84, 100–125 (1959). See Arnold, *supra* note 19, at 1313; Griswold, The Supreme Court 1959 Term—Foreword: Of Time and Attitudes—Professor Hart and Judge Arnold, 74 *Harv. L. Rev.* 81 (1960); Monaghan, Taking Supreme Court Opinions Seriously, 39 *Md. L. Rev.* 1, 16–25 (1979).

45. "The opinion must...be a coherent whole. All the parts must belong, all work together, and none be missing." White, Judicial Opinion and the Poem, *supra* note 7, at 1669, 1678.

46. See Posner, *supra* note 7, at 1391: Justice Stewart "will long best be remembered for having said of pornography [in his concurrence in *Jacobellis v. Ohio*, 378 U.S. 184, 197 (1964)] that he could not define it '[b]ut I know it when I see it, and the motion picture involved in this case is not that.' The candor and bluntness of this statement stood and stands in refreshing contrast to the characteristic evasions of the contemporary judicial style."

47. White, Judicial Opinion and the Poem, *supra* note 7, at 1679.

"I do not think we should lament the close divisions within the Court over the most difficult issues. I think we should instead welcome the opportunity that such divisions create for a dialogue within the Court that is visible outside its walls. I think a great opportunity is wasted when the justices talk past one another rather than grappling seriously with the divergent premises and perspectives that the nine of them bring to the interpretive mission. ... [T]he Constitution *itself* embodies a multitude of irreconcilable differences.

"Thus I believe that we should welcome forthright clashes within the Court and should resist anything that would tend to homogenize its membership or tilt the entire tribunal too uniformly in any one direction." Tribe, *supra* note 28, at 798 (emphasis in original).

48. *Miranda v. Arizona*, 384 U.S. 436, 508 (1965) (Harlan, J., dissenting).

49. See, e.g., Rehnquist, *supra* note 24, at 296.

"I know from the time during which I was an associate justice how important the assignment of the cases is to each member of the Court. The signed opinions produced by each justice are to a very large extent the only visible record of his work on the Court, and the office offers no greater reward than the opportunity to author an opinion on an important point of constitutional law. When I was an associate justice I eagerly awaited the assignments."

50. P. Freund, Introduction, in A. Bickel, *The Unpublished Opinions of Mr. Justice Brandeis* (1957), xvii.

51. Coffin, *supra* note 7, at 184.

52. Nesson, Mr. Justice Harlan, 85 *Harv. L. Rev.* 390, 391 (1971). "He believed firmly that a Court opinion should honestly explain the judgment." *Id.*

53. "For Brandeis almost the paramount quality of a good judge was the capacity to be reached by reason, the freedom from self-pride that without embarrassment permits a change of mind." Freund, *supra* note 50, at xx.

"The training of the judge, if coupled with what is styled the judicial temperament, will help in some degree to emancipate him from the suggestive power of individual dislikes and prepossessions. It will help to broaden the group to which his subconscious loyalties are due. Never will these loyalties be utterly extinguished while human nature is what it is." B. Cardozo, *The Nature of the Judicial Process* (1921), 176.

CASE INDEX

NAME INDEX

INDEX